TIPS FOR TANGLING

Information, ideas, exercises, and more to maximize your success in creating Zentangle® Art

TIPS FOR TANGLING

Information, ideas, exercises, and more to maximize your success in creating Zentangle® Art

Maureen Stott, CZT
Foreword by Cris Letourneau, CZT

Tips for Tangling
Information, ideas, exercises, and more to maximize your success in creating Zentangle® Art

by Maureen Stott, CZT

PUBLISHED BY
The Tao Of Tangling Publishing, Vernon, CT
www.Tao Of Tangling.com
ISBN: 978-0-692-03403-3

What CZTs are saying about this book

Tips for Tangling is not another book thrown out there that repeats the same information over and over using different words. This book takes the Zentangle method and focuses on the ways to be successful, no matter your intended application. Good for both beginners or more advanced tanglers, this book is a "must add to your collection." This will be one of the few books I recommend to students, because its value is as an enhancement to classes.

Kelly Barone, CZT

The information in this book presents the novice as well as the experienced artist with useful techniques to enhance their success in creating Zentangle art. The author's vast experience in teaching and creating bring an insight that proves to be extremely valuable. This is definitely a resource all tanglers should have in their library.

Donna Cyr, CZT

Tips for Tangling is a wonderful read for anyone who enjoys Zentangle. Maureen's tips and exercises throughout the book are helpful to folks who are new to Zentangle, experienced tanglers, and even experienced CZTs. There are a number of gems to be found within the book that will enhance your tangling experience. A great resource, with loads of information, to add to your library.

Tracy Lake, CZT

A comprehensive guide to tangling with excellent exercises for the novice and the more experienced tanglers.

Chari-Lynn R., CZT

I would recommend this book to CZTs and students alike. CZTs will be able to find interesting tidbits of info and suggestions to add to their classes. Tanglers, even if they have taken a class from a CZT, will find oodles of info that they might not get the chance to comprehend in a short class or that the teacher may not think to include. Breathing and mindfulness are explained very well as these are both important to the success of using the Zentangle Method. There are excellent tips on how to look after your tools and how to use different surfaces to find the most comfortable position. All in all, I would recommend this book as it is quite comprehensive in explaining just about everything a person practicing Zentangle would ever need.

Brenda Shaver, CZT

TABLE OF CONTENTS

Chapter 5 Play, Play, Play

Chapter 6 Time for Appreciation

Glossary

APPENDIX A

APPENDIX B

APPENDIX C

CRAZY
HUGGINS

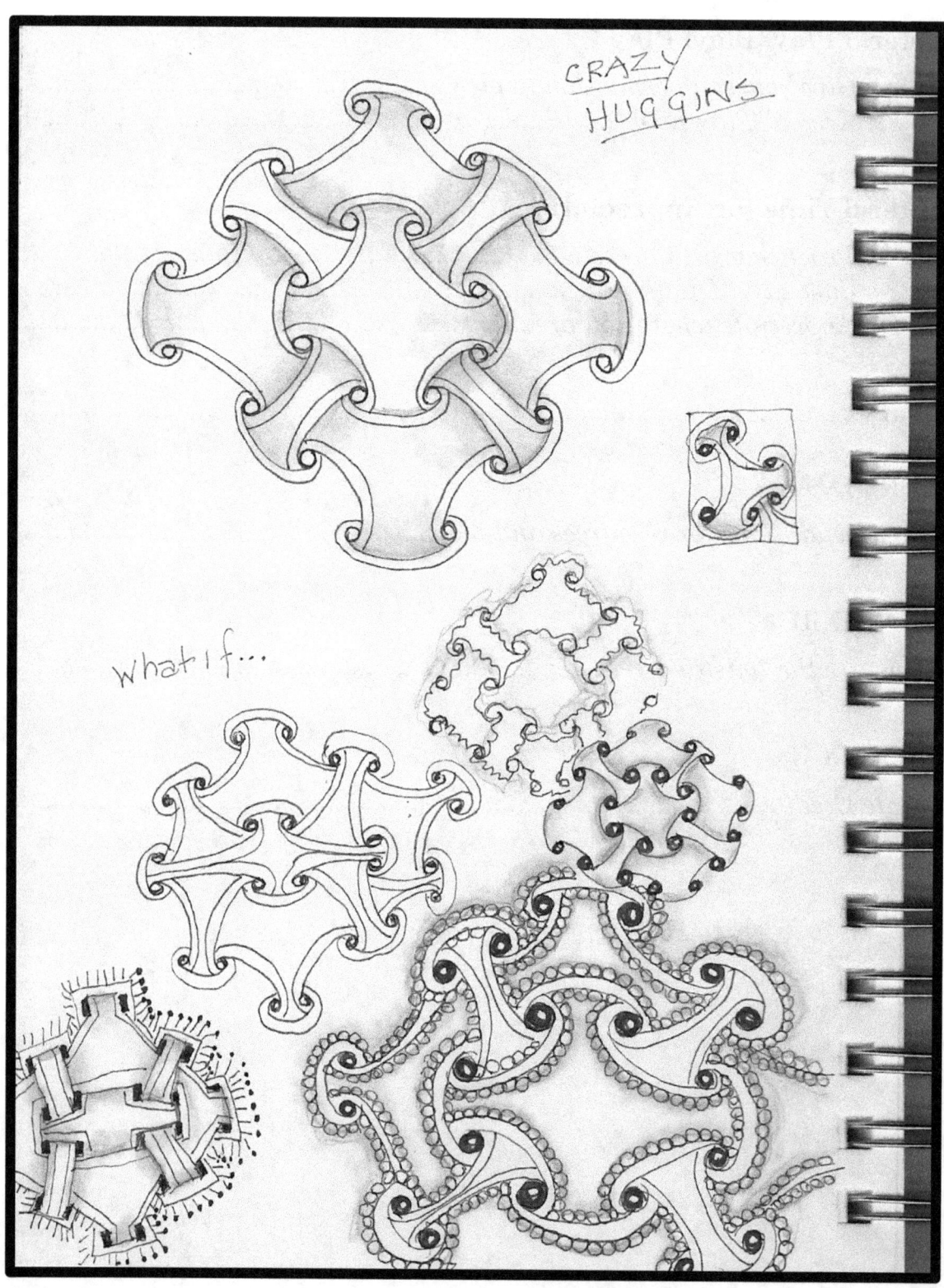

What if...

Foreword

by Cris Letourneau, author of *Made in the Shade* and *Pattern Play*

When I first discovered Zentangle in the fall of 2010, it was not the worldwide phenomenon it is today. In central Ohio, where I live, there was not a single Certified Zentangle Teacher (CZT) closer than 2 hours. There were no online classes. And there was only a single book in the library. This book was enough to get me thoroughly excited about this new way of making art, but all it did was pique my interest. I had to know more.

So, I immediately signed up to become a CZT. Three months later, I was listening to Rick Roberts and Maria Thomas, the founders of Zentangle, at the training and was astounded to realize just how much more there is to Zentangle than just making pretty pictures. In some ways, it was easier to learn about the Zentangle Method™ back then than it is now. While there is a lot more information online and in books today, not all of it is what Rick and Maria teach. There is much confusion about the difference between doodling and Zentangle. People tout "Zen Doodle" and self-proclaimed experts teach things so far away from the spirit of Zentangle that many students come to me confused and frustrated. They think they know Zentangle, but then realize that they have been misled. Even worse are the ones who never follow up with a CZT and are stuck in their misinformation.

This book fills a gap in the existing Zentangle literature. Instead of being just another pretty book with instructions on the art of Zentangle, it is full of tips from an experienced teacher who goes beyond just showing you how to draw tangles. Her friendly and engaging style makes you feel as though Maureen is sitting there with you and helping you get the most out of your tangling time.

The tips in this book offer the opportunity for you to tangle with ease as you enjoy the process of creating your tiles. It is a "must have" book to add to your library or to give to someone you know who enjoys tangling.

Introduction

Are you looking for ways to **tangle*** with more ease and joy? Are you looking for ways to work smarter, not harder? Are you looking for tips to create more confidently? Then this is the book for you. Whether you see yourself as a beginner or an experienced tangler — no matter what skill level — this book can help you develop your confidence as a **Zentangle**® artist.

When I'm teaching the **Zentangle Method**™ and someone seems to be struggling with an element, I ask myself, "What can I do to make this a bit easier?" As I work with the student and find a way to make it easier, I remember this for the next time I teach the class. Other tips come from years of being a calligrapher, a massage therapist, a teacher, and a CZT; some come from my own experiences with tangling; and some I discovered along my journey of life.

These tips are meant to be _tools_. If you need a screwdriver at this moment, you don't throw away all of your other tools, you put them aside until you need them. If you have a tool in your box but don't even know what it is, you keep it until you find out what it is and are ready to use it. We all know someone who has used a screwdriver (or perhaps a shoe) to hammer in a nail. While it works, it is not as efficient as a hammer and you have to work harder to get the job done. It is the same with these tips.

This book will also help you determine how you can work smarter, not harder. If a particular tip isn't a tool you want to embrace or try right now, set it aside until you are ready to use it.

Although this is not a book about how to draw patterns, it does contain illustrations of tiles and tangles. For those who would like to know the names of the tangles used in the artwork in the book, this information, along with the name of the person who created the tangle, can be found in Appendix C.

For the exercises in the book that use a **tile** you can use official tiles with the red Zentangle logo on the back, artist tiles offered by other companies, or you can cut your own tiles from quality art paper. When the exercise indicates that you need a pen, you can use the traditional pen for **Zentangle Art**™, which is a Sakura® Pigma® Micron® 01 pen or a similar fine-point ink pen. The Sakura pens are often referred to as Micron followed by the **nib** number such as Micron 01 or Micron 08. If the exercise indicates a pencil, use a number 2 or HB pencil.

*_Glossary Words are shown in_ **bold** _when first used._

As with all art, the quality of the materials contributes to the quality of the finished product. If you are working on a piece that you want to last a long time, be sure to use **archival** paper and pens. This means that the paper and pens are acid-free and have permanence. All of the official Zentangle tiles are archival paper and the Sakura Micron pens contain archival ink.

For those of you who have decided to come on this path and discover what works for you, Thank You and Happy Tangling!

Maureen

www.TaoOfTangling.com
Maureen@TaoOfTangling.com

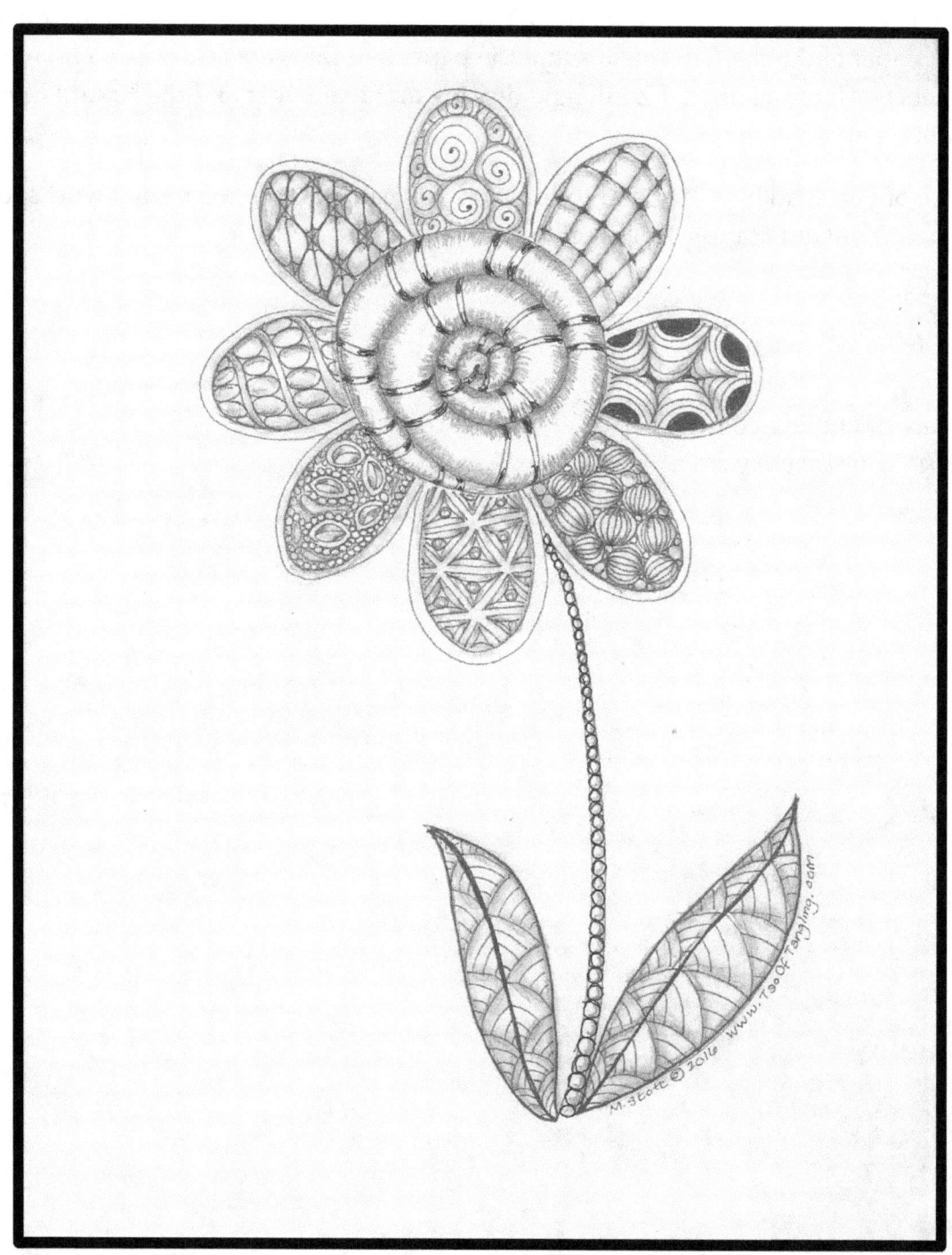

Chapter 1
Before You Begin Tangling

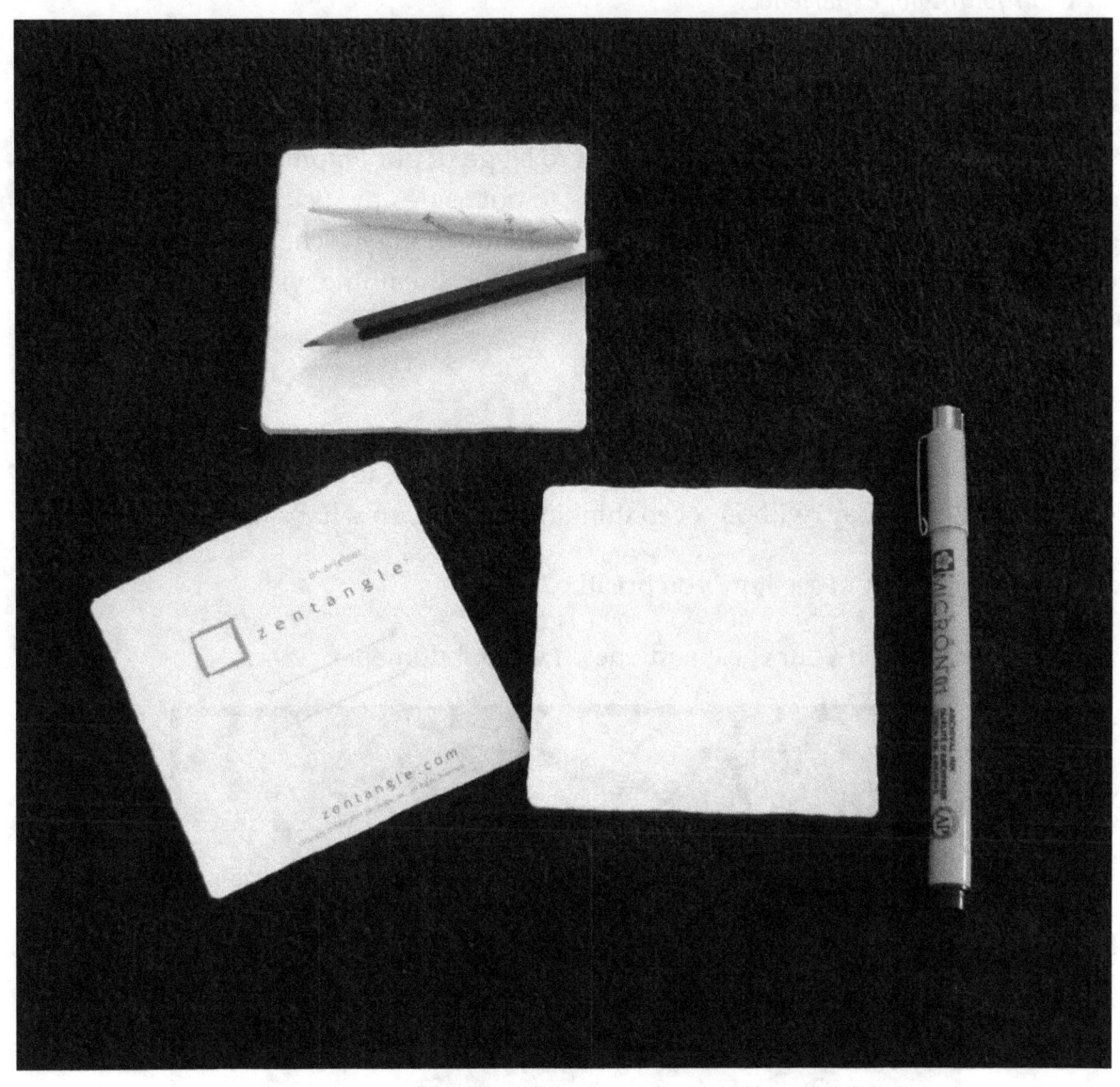

Tip 1: Prepare your mind before picking up your pencil

"[Mindfulness is...] the awareness that emerges through paying attention on purpose, in the present moment, and non-judgmentally to the unfolding of experience."

Jon Kabbat-Zinn's definition of Mindfulness

Before we start to work on a tile, it is helpful to let go of our "**monkey mind**" so we can focus on one stroke at a time. In other words, to put aside any distracting thoughts in our heads and allow ourselves to be totally present in the moment. There are many ways to accomplish this. For this tip we will look at just a few: breathing, visualization, counting backwards, and music.

Breathing

The easiest way to become present is to take some deep breaths. Sounds easy, doesn't it? We all breathe every day, without even thinking about it, so what's the big deal?

Here is an experiment to see how you breathe. Ready?

1. Put one hand on your chest and one on your abdomen.

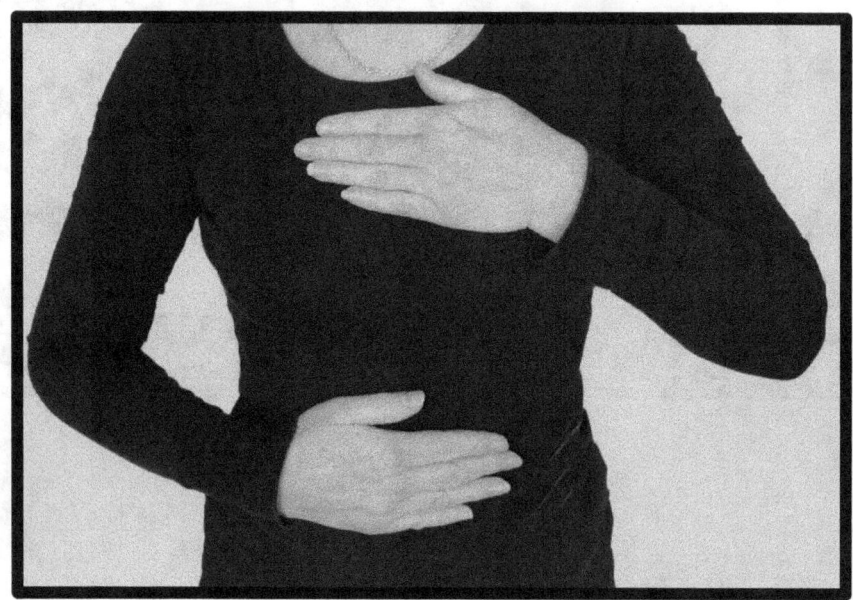

2. As you breathe in and out, notice which hand moves. If you cannot tell, or if the hand on your chest moves more, you are doing what is called "shallow breathing." Many of us go through life using shallow breaths.

3. Next, put both hands on your ribs.

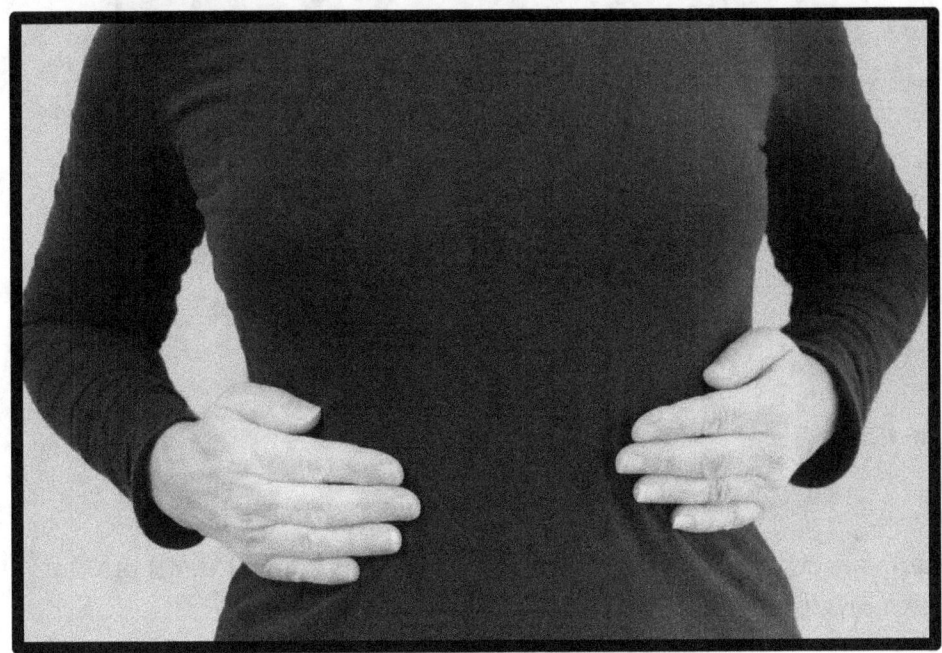

4. This time when you inhale, use your breath to move your ribs, which in turn will move your hands. Exhale when you are ready. To move your ribs, you need to let your stomach muscles relax.

When you move your ribs with your breath, that is called "deep breathing," "belly breathing," or "deep belly breathing."

Have you ever watched a baby breathe? Their little bellies go up and down with each inhalation and exhalation. To get more oxygen through your system and to your brain, strive to do the same thing.

Practice belly breathing whenever you think of it. You may want to make a habit of taking three deep belly breaths each time you stop for a red light. With practice, deep breathing becomes as natural a way of breathing for you as it is to a newborn baby.

Visualization

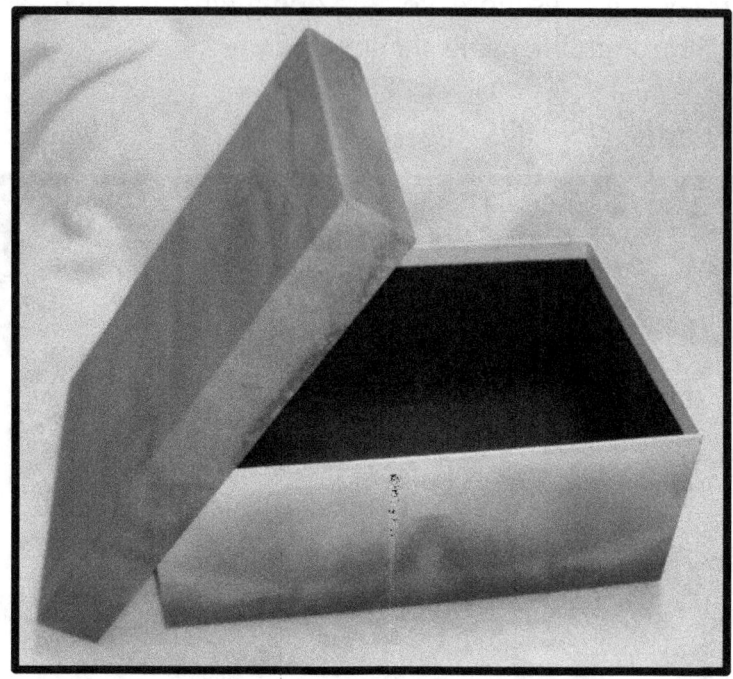

An easy visualization is to imagine an empty box on your lap. Put all of your current concerns, questions, thoughts, feelings, and emotions in the box.

Now mentally take that box and imagine putting it on a closet shelf where it will stay until you are done tangling. When you have finished tangling, if you desire, you can go back and take the box off the shelf and restore all of the current concerns, questions, thoughts, feelings, and emotions that you put there.

Counting backwards

Another way to quiet your mind is to close your eyes and very, very slowly count backwards from five. With each number, you relax a different part of your body starting at the top of your head and ending at the soles of your feet. As you count down, feel the muscles get heavy and your tension melt away.

Start by finding a comfortable seated position and gently closing your eyes or gazing down toward the floor.

When you breathe, inhale through your nose slowly (3 - 4 seconds) and then take twice as long to exhale through your mouth (6 - 8 seconds).

4

Each time you say the number aloud or in your head, breathe in and relax the associated body parts on the exhale. Feel your muscles in that area relax more and more with each subsequent breath. After saying each number three times or when you feel that you have released as much tension as possible, go on to the next number.

Take a breath and begin the countdown.

- **Five** - With each slow exhale feel the muscles in your *scalp, ears,* and *face* melt more and more. Let your **chin** go slack. Take a deep belly breath in and slowly exhale.

- **Four** - With each slow exhale feel the muscles in your *neck, shoulders*, *arms*, and *hands* get heavier and heavier. Feel your shoulders drop. Take a deep belly breath in and slowly exhale.

- **Three** - Continue with the muscles in your *torso* and *hips*, remembering to use three slow, deep belly breaths as you relax your muscles, ending with a deep breath in and slowly exhale.

- **Two** - Continue with the muscles in your *thighs* and *knees*, breathe.

- **One** - Continue with the muscles in your *calves, feet, toes,* and the *soles of your feet*.

- Take one more slow, deep belly breath and as you exhale, slowly open your eyes. Ahhhh....

You may want to record yourself saying each step and then listen to the recording to avoid the distraction of having to read what comes next. After doing this exercise over time you won't need the recording. As you say or think the number and breathe your muscles will start to relax.

Music

Music can have a calming effect that many people find contributes to their ability to get into the "Zen" space. There are many recordings that may help you relax. Some categories include: classical music, easy listening, new age, meditation, spa music, etc. You'll probably want to avoid music with someone singing words. If it is a song that you know, you may find yourself singing along with the artist and therefore not focused on your tangling.

If you don't know where to start, see Appendix A for a list of my favorite artists/albums.

And now you have some ways to let go, relax, and get ready to tangle. Try one or try them all. Find what works for you.

Tip 2: Slo-o-o-o-ow down! Work mindfully!

Tangling is more beneficial when done slowly and mindfully. To see the impact of working slowly, try this exercise.

First, gather the following materials. You will need:

- Two 3½" square pieces of nice white drawing paper or white Zentangle tiles
- A pencil
- A fine-point ink pen, such as a Sakura® Pigma® Micron® 01 pen *(also referred to as a Micron 01 pen)*
- A piece of scrap paper

1. On the scrap of paper, write down the names of four tangles that you are very familiar with and can draw without thinking about what stroke comes next.

2. With the pencil, draw a dot in each of the four corners of one of the tiles and draw a frame or border.

3. With the pencil, draw a light line that divides the tile into four sections. In Zentangle terminology this line is called a "**string**." For example, you could use the letter "N" (aka the "Z" string):

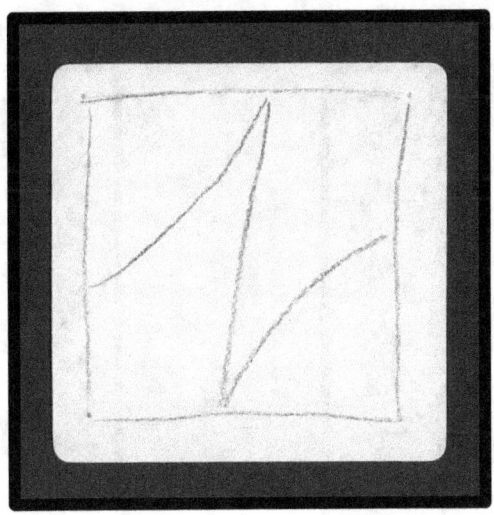

(Note: This string is drawn darker for clarity in the photo. When you are drawing it, draw it lightly so it fades into the background when you add the tangles.)

4. Draw the same frame and string on the second tile. Both tiles will look similar at this point.

5. Using your list of four tangles, (*I am using Crescent Moon, Hollibaugh, Cadent, and Quipple*) decide which tangle to put in each of the four sections of one of these tiles.

6. Using the pen, complete each section on the first tile *as quickly as you can* without any focus or intent.

7. On the other tile, use your pen to draw the *same* tangles in the same sections, but this time breathe, and with focus and deliberate strokes *slowly* draw each tangle one stroke at a time.

8. Put them side by side so you can compare them.

If you are like most people, drawing quickly without focus *felt* different from drawing slowly with focus. Were you aware of these differences?

When we are focused and draw the patterns with deliberate strokes, working one stroke at a time, making it the best stroke that we can, it is evident in our art. It results in **tangle elements** (*i.e., lines, curved lines, dots, "S" lines, and orbs*) with a different quality. Many people report that when they are more interested in seeing what the artwork will look like than they are in the process, they tend to do the strokes quickly. Which of the two tiles below do you think was drawn slowly?

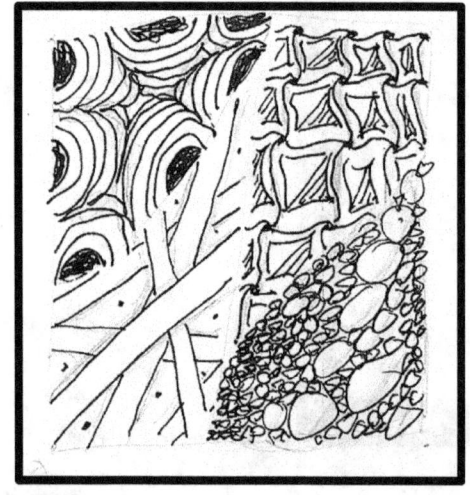

TILE A

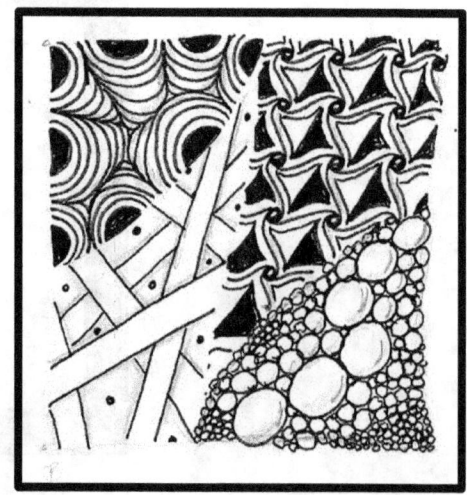

TILE B

Did you pick Tile B?

The speed with which you make your strokes also changes the style of the lines you draw. To see this, try the next experiment:

You will need:

- A Micron 01 or other fine-point pen
- A piece of scrap paper

1. **Slowly** and deliberately draw a few lines on the scrap paper using your Micron pen or a similar pen. **Remember to breathe.**

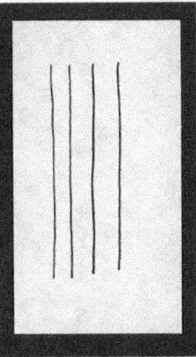

2. Next, try to duplicate the lines working **quickly.** You can't, right? Lines with these qualities can be achieved only if you work slowly and intentionally, focusing on one stroke at a time.

3. Now let's see what happens if you draw a few lines very quickly, still working with intention. To produce these quick lines, place your pen on the paper and then flick your wrist. Try flicking toward you, away from you, and horizontally to see what works for you.

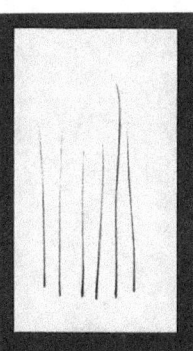

Can you see how the strokes start dark and end up lighter? If you try to draw this slowly you will find that the quality of these lines can be achieved only if the strokes are drawn quickly.

Not every line needs to be drawn with the speed of a proverbial turtle. Draw each stroke with awareness, at a speed that is comfortable for you to achieve the effect that you intend.

You may find that some tangles require a quick stroke or strokes. The tile below includes two such tangles. The top left tangle, Flwr Box, uses short quick strokes for the lines in the petals and the bottom right tangle, B'Dylan, uses a series of longer quick strokes.

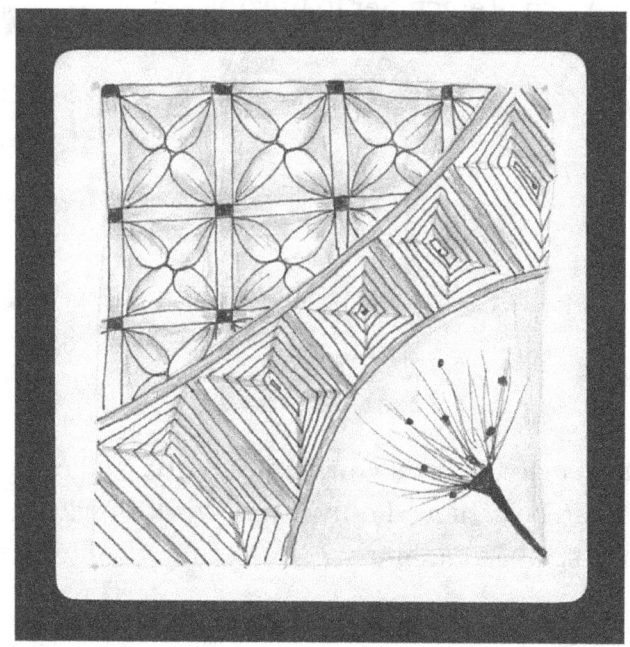

Tip 3: Don't worry about being perfect

"It's not always easy to let go of the perfectionism, conclusions or frustration stopping what is possible... but it's always more joyful when you do!"

Blossom Benedict, Access Consciousness

If you lived before machines produced goods, you did not expect anything in your house to look like anything else. Your bowl would not look like my bowl. Your chair would not look just like my chair. Everything was handmade. Items might be similar, but not exactly alike.

Machines make it possible for the end products to be predictable and consistent — every dinner plate in a set looks like every other dinner plate in that set; every kitchen chair looks just like the others in the set, etc. Soon the idea of perfection in creating became the standard.

When you are tangling, do you believe that perfect means better? Do you hold onto the belief that if your art isn't "perfect" it is somehow unworthy? What if this is all a myth? One of the joys of Zentangle art and **Zentangle Inspired Art (ZIA)** is that it is non-representational. It is not meant to "look like" something. It is a simply a series of strokes.

When I was a growing up, every Christmas our mother gave my brothers and me hand-knit sweaters. I remember one year when I saw a mistake in the pattern. When I brought it to Mom's attention she lovingly responded, "If you want it perfect buy it in a store. The mistake shows that this sweater was made with love. You can't buy that!"

The Zentangle Method teaches us that there are no mistakes, just opportunities. How many of us truly understand this and completely embrace the concept? I didn't at first. If the tangle didn't come out exactly as the picture of the **step-outs** it was a "mistake." Have you ever had a certain tangle in mind and when you started to draw it found that it didn't match the one in the book or the one in your head? Did you judge it as unworthy and discard the tile without finishing it? I used to do that.

Now I think about the pearls of wisdom I heard years ago in a calligraphy class:

> When you create your work you have in your mind what you want your artwork to look like. When it doesn't match what is in your mind you judge it as inadequate, wrong, a mistake, or ugly. When someone else sees what you have created they do not have any preconceived images in their head. They see it as it is. They can appreciate the beauty of the art that you are denying.

Want more evidence that what we judge to be unworthy is really only in our own minds? I remember reading about a woman who has a medical condition that affects her fine motor skills so when she tangles all of her elements are shaky — especially her lines and orbs. At first she was frustrated trying to do what her body would not allow. Then she turned that around and rather than seeing her art as unworthy, created art where her shaky tangle elements became part of the pattern and her trademark. She turned her "lemons into lemonade." To get a *slight* idea of what this might feel like, try creating a tile with your non-dominant hand.

Not only is it an exercise in letting go of perfectionism, working with your non-dominant hand forces you to work more slowly and deliberately. You don't hold an expectation that it is going to be up to your usual standards so you just do your best and enjoy the experience. Isn't that interesting?

Tip 4: Take a class from a Certified Zentangle Teacher

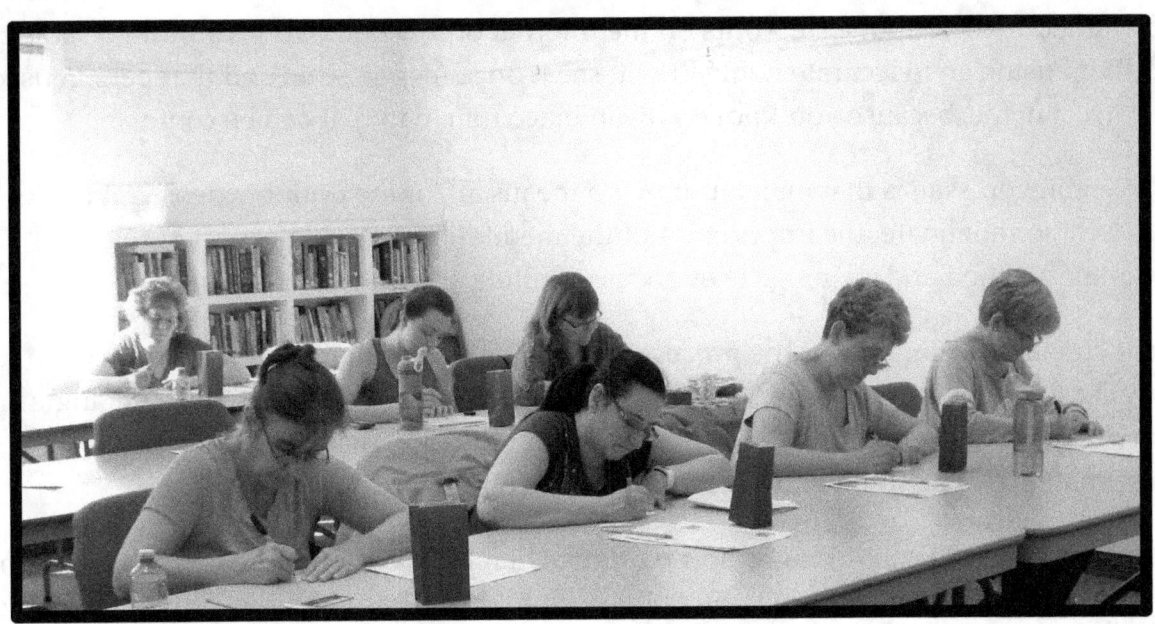

My first career was that of a musician and music teacher. I would have students coming for private lessons who were self-taught. Often these students had formed bad habits that were very difficult, and in some cases impossible, to change.

I started doing Zentangle art using the information I found on the Internet and from the books I bought. After a short time I took my first Zentangle class to make sure that I wasn't forming bad habits. I was hooked. And as they say, "The rest is history."

Someone recently asked, *"Why should I spend money for a class when there is so much free information online and I can learn it by watching videos and reading books?"*

Well, you can learn how to draw patterns using the online information and books. What you don't get online and in books is the Zentangle® Method. There is so much more to Zentangle art than putting patterns together on a piece of paper. There are *many* books written by people who are not trained in this art form. If you are buying a book, please make sure that it is written by a **Certified Zentangle Teacher (CZT™)**.

For someone who has not taken a class, it can be very difficult to know if the information on the Internet or in books is accurate. I recently viewed a video about Zentangle art that contained misinformation, including incorrect names of tangles. Why is that important? If you wanted to look up the step-outs on the Internet or in a book you wouldn't be able to find them using an inaccurate name. If you see it on someone's tile and that person used the correct name, because you know it by an inaccurate name, it can be confusing.

An even bigger issue is that many, but by no means all, of the online videos and books gloss over, or eliminate, the importance of the meditative, relaxing aspect of the Zentangle Method and training. They focus on filling spaces with patterns.

When creating Zentangle art, the *process* is more important than the end product. Learning to do the strokes in a focused, mindful way is what differentiates Zentangle art from doodling and from other art forms. It doesn't make Zentangle art any better or worse than doodling or other art forms, just different.

So, if your goal is to copy designs and patterns, then learning from the Internet and books may fill your requirement. But if you truly want to do art based on the Zentangle Method and reap all the benefits it provides, it is important that you take a class from a Certified Zentangle Teacher (CZT) and learn the whole process. To see if there is a CZT in your area, look on the official website: *www.zentangle.com/teachers.php*.

Chapter 2
While You Are Creating

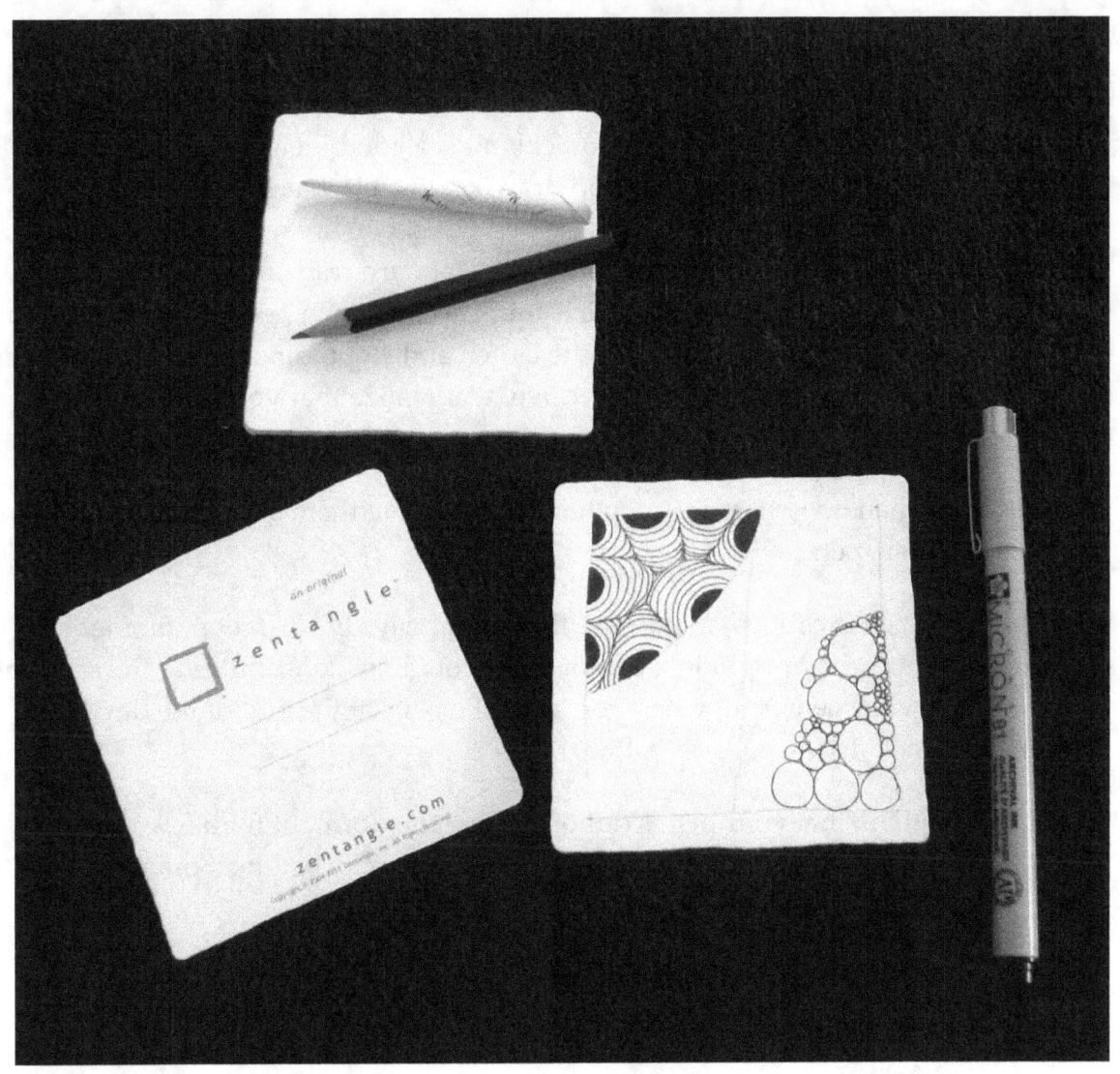

Tip 5: Take care of your pen

Zentangle art is drawn on a white tile with black ink. The traditional pen is a Pigma® Micron® 01 pen by Sakura because it works well with the print-making paper of the official tiles and the ink is **archival**, which means that it will last a long time. I recently read a blog posting where a woman stated that her Micron pens were not lasting long and others concurred. Although they do not last indefinitely, there may be ways to prolong the life of your Micron pens.

- Are you putting the cap on tightly when you are not actually drawing with the pen? Uncapped pens dry out more quickly. It is a good idea to get in the habit of capping your pen *every* time you stop drawing, even if that is only a few minutes, until you are automatically capping the pen when you are not drawing. It is similar to learning how to drive a car with a standard transmission. In the beginning you have to concentrate and think about which pedal to push with each foot plus get the timing of releasing the clutch and stepping on the gas. After some point in time that you don't even perceive, you realize that you are doing all of it without thinking.

- Keep more than one Micron 01 pen handy and rotate them so you are not always using the same pen.

- When your pen is capped, make sure that it is always lying flat on its side. Keeping your pens upright in a cup or other container contributes to the shortened life span of your pen. And, when you store the pens at the end of the day, put them in a cool, dry area.

- When you think that your pen is out of ink let it lie dormant for a few days, keeping it on its side. When you pick it up again, it may be fine. Sometimes this works, sometimes it doesn't.

- Use your Micron 01 pens for drawing and small detail work. Use a Micron 05 or 08 to fill in black background areas unless they are small.

- Try writing with the pen at a 90-degree angle and see if that helps. In the 1980's Micron pens were designed to be disposable technical pens. People who used them for technical drawings used them at 90 degrees, so the **nib** is designed for that angle. If you find that your nib is wearing out, this may help.

- The paper you use can affect the life of your pen. Inexpensive paper often has a rougher surface than the paper used for the official tiles. This coarse surface can cause the nib to wear down faster. While it may not feel rough to your touch, if you compare it to a smoother, usually more expensive, paper or an official tile you can usually feel the difference.

- I bought an inexpensive sketchbook so I could play with different tangles and **tangleations** and found that it has rougher paper. I decided to use a less expensive pen when working in the sketchbook and to save my Micron pens for tiles and my sketchbooks with paper of higher quality. At first I used an extra fine Sharpie pen but it bled through the inexpensive paper to the other side of the page. Now I use an an inexpensive, fine-point black gel pen when tangling in this sketchbook.

- Are you using the pen to write on surfaces other than paper? If you are using your Micron pen to tangle a sea shell, for example, you may find that it grinds down the nib very quickly. Even if your pen seems to "work" on a different surface, if it is affecting your Micron pen it is better to find a more suitable writing tool for that material. You can create Zentangle art anywhere and on any surface if you have the right tool.

- Keep a piece of scrap paper handy to test your pens and to warm up before putting pen to tile. If possible, use the same paper as the tile you are using.

- Are the nibs of your pen bent? Check the amount of pressure you are using while you draw. *(More about pressure in Tip 7: Draw with a relaxed hand.)* If you continue to experience a bent nib, see if using a larger nib pen such as a Micron 03 or 05 makes it easier to write with a lighter touch.

Vive La Pen!

Tip 6: Turn your tile; pull the pen

One of the basic techniques of Zentangle art is to turn your tile as you are drawing your tangles. This technique is so simple, it is often forgotten. Because the tiles are small, it is easy to draw a line, for example, without turning the tile.

When you are drawing on the tile, the pen moves more easily if you pull the pen toward you. By turning the tile, this is easy to do. When we push the pen to create a stroke it sometimes gets caught on the fibers of the paper and may produce a shaky line. Think of a rock rolling down a hill. Letting it go down the hill is easy. Pushing it up the hill takes more effort.

Some tanglers have a habit of drawing lines horizontally. While there is no rule that says that you can't draw lines horizontally, try turning your tile and drawing those same lines pulling the pen toward you. If you have been drawing your lines horizontally for awhile when you first pull the pen toward you it may feel strange. With practice you may find that you prefer to pull your strokes.

Tip 7: Draw with a relaxed hand

Do you find yourself shaking out your writing hand or noticing that it is cramped or achy when working on a tile or after completing it? If so, check to see how hard you are gripping your pen. If your grip is too tight the muscles in your hand will become fatigued and sore. Here is an exercise to see what it feels like to use different grips and to discover how lightly you can hold your pen and still produce confident-looking strokes.

You will need:

- A Pigma® Micron® 01 or other fine-point pen
- A piece of scrap paper

Using the piece of scrap paper, vary the grip of your pen as you draw a series of lines. Start by lightly holding the pen as you draw a line. Then, grip it tighter and tighter with each subsequent line.

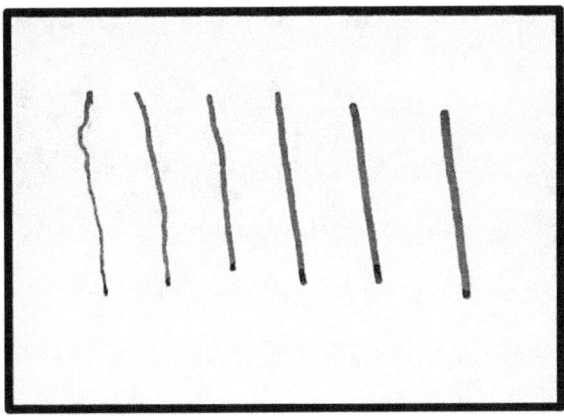

Did you feel the difference in your hand when you gripped the pen lightly and really, really tight? Do you see a difference in your lines? Did you find that as you gripped the pen tighter you pressed into the paper more? Some people grip the pen tightly without adding extreme pressure, so your lines may not look like mine. Because the ink flows so easily from a Micron pen, it is best to write with pressure that is little more than the weight of the pen.

Find the grip that gives you confident tangle elements without strain in your hand and, over time, you may find that a lighter touch works better.

Sometimes when you are focusing on the pattern being drawn, you may slip into a tight grip again. If that happens, try holding something in your non-dominant hand such as a pencil, stress ball, crumpled up paper towel, etc. When you notice that your writing hand grip is increasing, squeeze the object in your non- dominant hand, which in turn eases the grip on your pen as if by magic. You may find that, over time, as you build **muscle memory**, your hand stays relaxed without needing to grasp the object.

Note: If you continue to have problems with your hands, thumbs, or fingers don't ignore the signs. Please consult the health care provider responsible for your health to make sure that it isn't something serious.

Tip 8: Look ahead

Musicians often need to "sight read" a piece of music. In other words, they are required to play or sing music that they have never seen before, without practicing it first. Sight reading trains the musician to look ahead to the notes that are coming up and lets their fingerings or voice follow. We use this skill of looking ahead when we play music, read words, drive, etc. It is also a skill that is helpful when drawing tangles.

While drawing a stroke, let your eye focus slightly ahead of the end of the pen. Practice letting your eye guide your hand and pen to where you intend your pen stroke to go. See how far ahead you can look and still feel confident in your strokes. One way to practice this is to play with the following exercise.

You will need:

- A pencil
- A Pigma® Micron® 01 or other fine-point pen
- A piece of scrap paper

1. Using your pencil, draw a dot near the top of the paper and a second dot approximately two or three inches down from and in line with the first dot.

2. Place your pen on the top dot. While looking at the bottom dot, draw your line to the bottom dot.

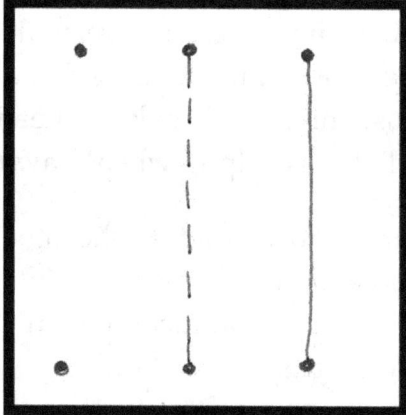

3. Repeat the exercise with your pencil dots farther apart to see how far you can look ahead and get the results you desire.

Tip 9: Don't throw away any tiles

Before reading further, look at these three tiles.

Tile 1

Tile 2

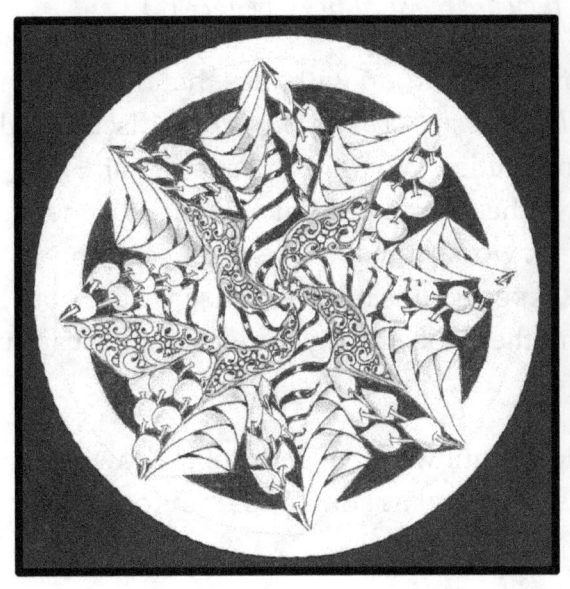

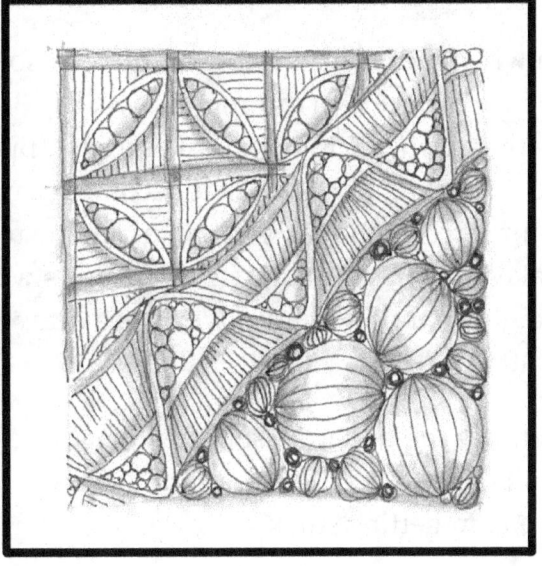

Tile 3

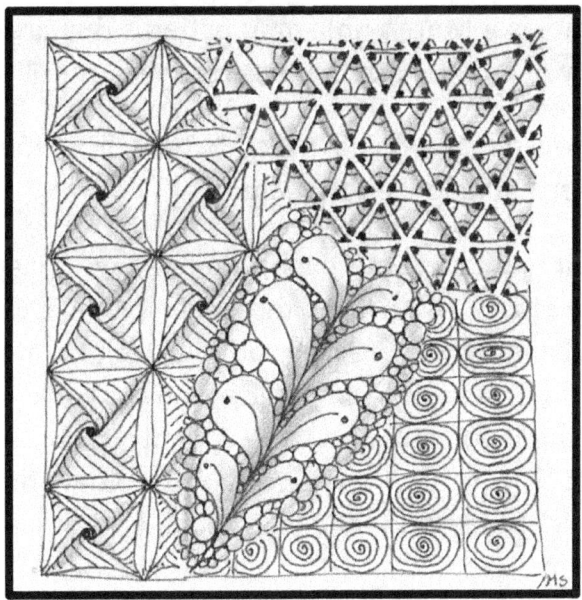

These tiles contain what some tanglers would call a "mistake" because there are unintentional strokes or something not quite as expected. Can you find the unintentional area in each tile?

These tiles show that what we, the artist, judge to be a glaring mistake goes unnoticed by many viewers. *(If you don't see the "mistakes," they are revealed in Appendix B.)*

Even when we create a tile mindfully we sometimes end up with tiles that do not come out as we expected in our mind's eye. Tip 3: *Don't worry about being perfect* discussed the concept that there are no mistakes, only opportunities. What this means is that if you make an unintentional mark it becomes part of the overall pattern and because the image is non-representational, you can make the mark work for you. Thus, there are no mistakes. When we do not get the results we expected it is often because we are not making the strokes mindfully, we are drawing them too quickly, or we are just learning the pattern.

Sometimes the pattern just needs to be practiced until we are comfortable drawing it. When I need to practice a pattern, I draw it as large and as slowly as I can to discover where I am getting stuck.

I have had students come to me and ask for my help figuring out a pattern. Sometimes, their frustration isn't what they are or are not doing, it is the pattern itself. As Zentangle art gains popularity, some people are publishing patterns that are complex and representational. Be wary of any pattern that has many or complicated steps.

Not everyone will enjoy every tangle. That's okay! The world would be a very boring place if everyone and everything looked the same.

Many of us have tiles that don't meet our expectations so we consider them less than acceptable. We've all been there, right? I call these tiles *"For My Eyes Only"* or *FMEO* tiles. Don't get rid of them! Whenever you are tempted to pretend that a tile never existed and throw it in the recycle bin or discard pile, put a date on the back and put it away for a day or two. Look at it again and if you still don't like it, wait a month. Often things look better in hindsight. If you don't like the tile, it may mean that you are not finished yet. It may never turn into your favorite tile, and that's okay. So, take out your "For My Eyes Only" (FMEO) tiles and use them.

What can you do with them? Here are some suggestions:

- Save them. When you look at them months later, they are a reminder of how far you have come.

- Use them when you want to experiment with a new product, pen, or technique before committing to a new blank tile.

- Study them. See if you can take the part that you find displeasing and change it into something different — something you like.

- Share them. Do you know someone else who tangles? You might be surprised to find that the tile that your friend sees as a FMEO is beautiful to you just the way it is — and vice versa.

- Share them with someone who does not tangle. You make them happy and you never have to see the tile again.

- Exchange FMEO tiles with other tanglers. Challenge them to redo the tile and find a way to change it from an FMEO to one for everyone's eyes.

- Above all...enjoy these tiles again.

Tip 10: Write notes on the back of your tiles

Whether you are creating a new tile, experimenting with a new tangle, or trying a new technique, be sure to put descriptive notes on the back of the tile so you have them for future reference.

At some point you may decide to use a new technique or add color to your tiles. It is frustrating to go back to a tile and not be able to remember which products you used, or which colors you used to get that wonderful shade of green. Even if you didn't like the way the tangle, technique, or tile looked, keep the notated tile so that the next time you want to repeat the tangle, technique, or color you'll know what didn't work and can choose something different.

It is helpful to include the names of all of the tangles you used, unless they are the tangles you use over and over and you know their names without thinking. (These patterns are known as our **"Mac and Cheese"** tangles because they are our "comfortable" patterns.) Sometimes I even note the names of my favorite tangles because I can't always remember how to spell the names.

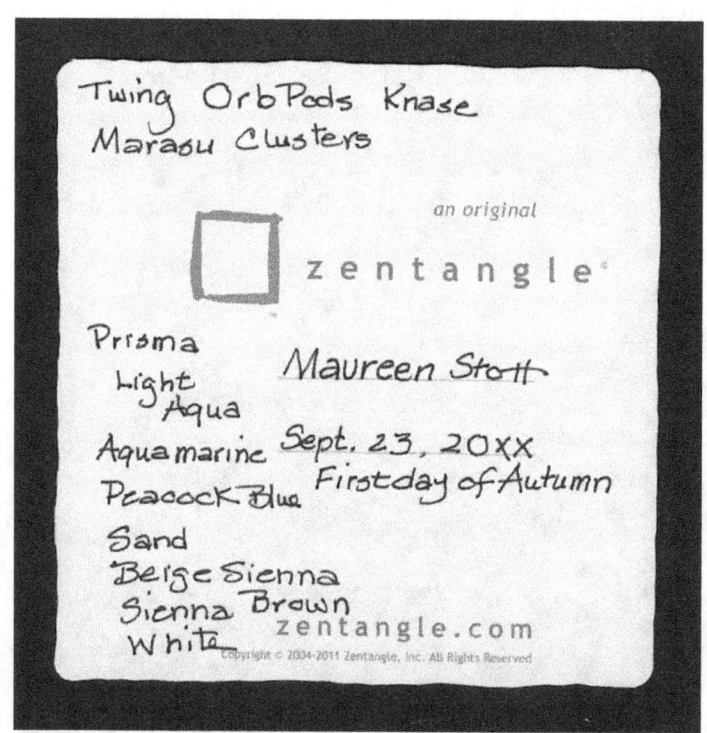

With so many tangles available on the Internet, it is easy to use a tangle and then forget about it for awhile. By the time you use it again it may be difficult to remember the name of the tangle or the site where you found it. Without the name of a tangle it is impossible to look up the step-outs. If you have written the name of the tangle on the back of a tile, it saves a lot of time and frustration.

Tip 11: It's okay to put tiles away uncompleted

Do you feel compelled to complete your tiles in one sitting? If you are not satisfied with the way a tile is progressing, or you don't know what tangle to put in a section, put the tile aside and come back to it at a later date.

When you pick it up again and look at it with fresh eyes, it will probably look different to you. If you struggled with which tangle to draw next, when you look at it a second time the sequence of tangles may become clearer than before.

Have you considered that your tile might be complete? Leaving white space can add to the drama of a tile. When we first learn Zentangle basics we fill up every space on the tile with a pattern. On the first tile we use a string to divide the tile into sections and then draw a pattern in each section. This procedure is used to illustrate some of the basic concepts of Zentangle art, to give structure while creating the spontaneous art form, and to help us get over our fear of "doing it wrong." As we have seen, there is no "wrong."

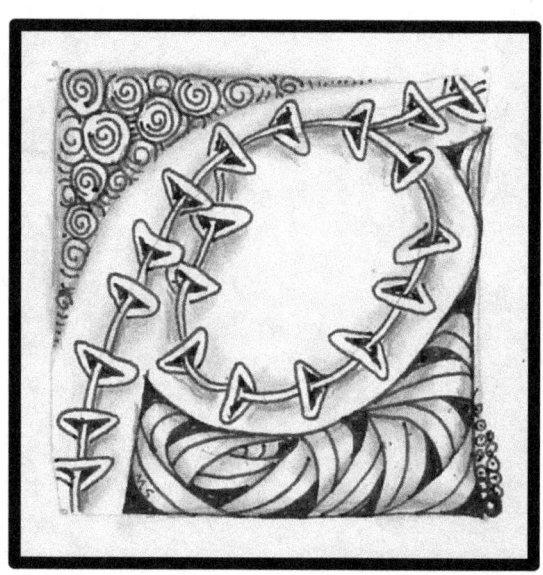

It is a good exercise to leave empty space on your tile. This is more easily said than done. Many of us find it uncomfortable to leave empty white spaces on the tile. Empty space is not the enemy. White space gives the eye a place to rest.

Chapter 3
Tips For Drawing Tangle Elements

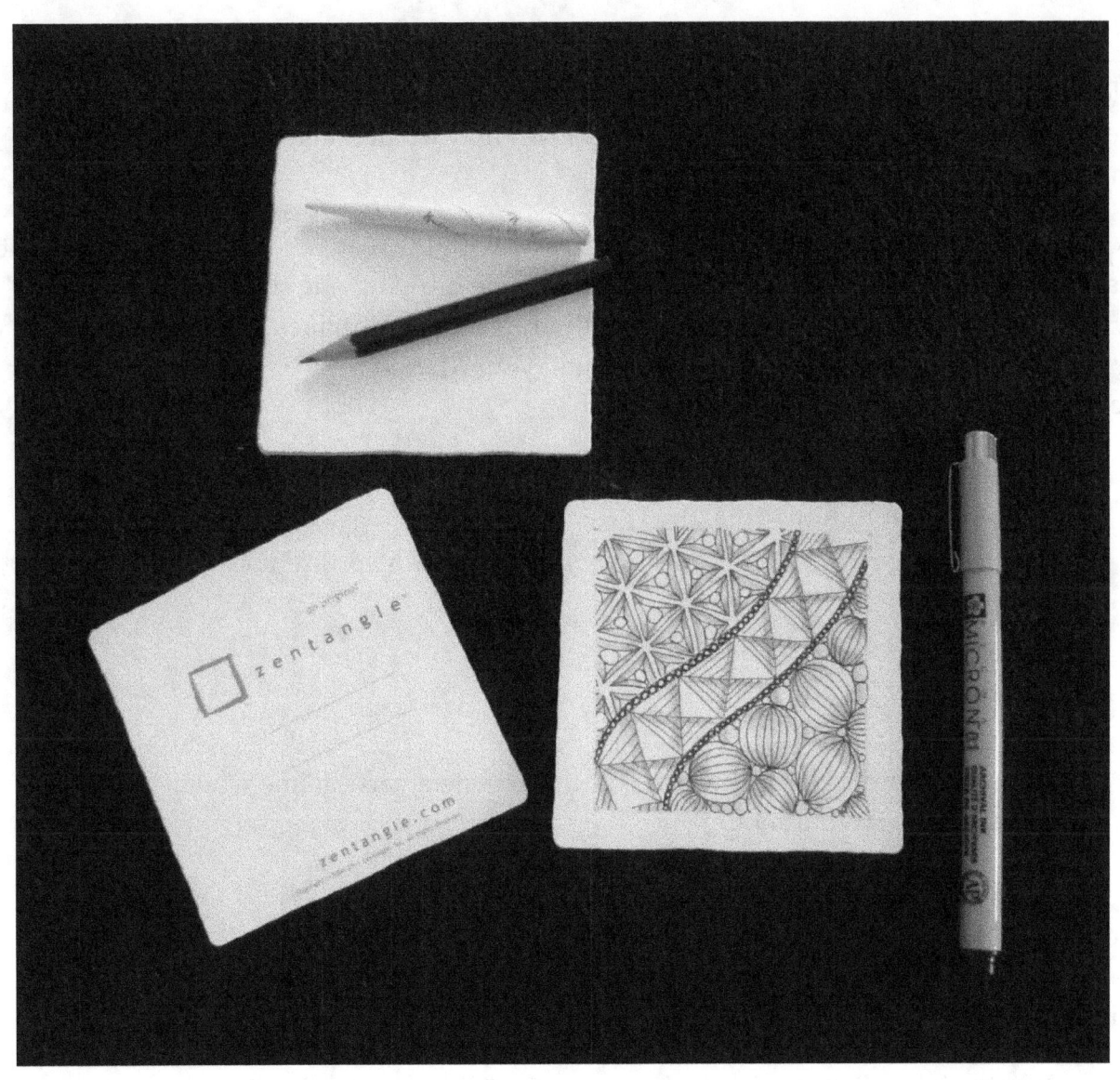

Tip 12: All lined up

If you cannot draw a straight line then Zentangle art is the perfect art form for you.

When you are tangling, straight lines on a tile don't have to be drawn "perfectly straight." We are humans and our imperfections are the charm of art. Learning to live with imperfectly straight lines is part of learning to accept our own limitations and enjoy our art.

However, if you would like your lines to be a bit straighter, the first question to ask yourself is, "Am I going too fast?" Slowing down may be all it takes to make your lines more pleasing to your eye.

A former student told me that she was not happy with the way her tiles were coming out. I asked her if she was remembering to breathe while drawing one stroke at a time. She wasn't. What does breathing have to do with drawing straight lines? Would you be willing to do an experiment using your breath, your Micron pen (or a similar pen) and a scrap of paper?

- Take a deep belly breath in through your nose (inhale) and slowly breathe out through your mouth (exhale).
- On the next breath, while you slowly *inhale,* draw a vertical line on the scrap paper.
- Put your pen down as you *exhale*.
- Take another breath or two.
- Now, pick up your pen again.
- Take another deep belly breath. This time create a vertical line while you slowly *exhale* through your mouth.

Looking at the two lines, do you notice a difference? If you are like most people, it is easier to draw a straighter line as you exhale. The resulting line is subtly (or for some, dramatically) straighter and more confident.

When I do the inhalation portion of this experiment, I have a tendency to draw my vertical line from the bottom of the paper to the top. This creates a line that is wobbly and tentative. Did you experience that too? I find that it also helps me to draw straighter lines if I turn the tile so that I am pulling the vertical stroke from the top of the tile toward me as I exhale.

Not only does this "pen to paper on the exhalation" contribute to the quality of the stroke, it also helps us to slow down, relax, and enjoy the process. When we create mindfully, the process becomes magical, with the end result being a beautiful piece of art.

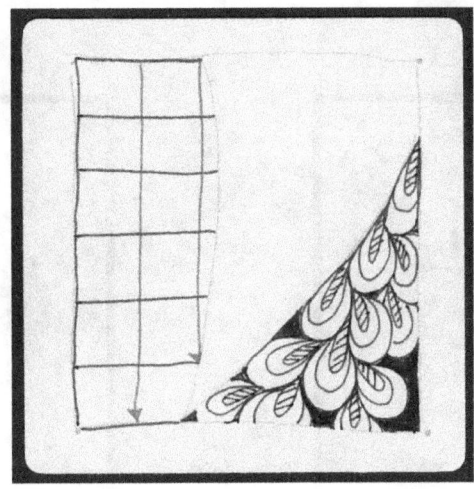

As you draw your favorite tangle patterns, remember to do each stroke on a slow exhalation with your eye guiding your pen *(For more information about guiding your pen, see Tip 8: Look ahead)*

Tip 13: Aura-ing around the tangle

When you are drawing auras you are outlining a tangle or tangle elements. This includes the space between tangle elements, known as **negative space**. Tile 1 below shows the tangle "Pokeleaf." Tile 2 shows an **aura** drawn between the pokeleaf highlighting the negative space. Tile 3 shows this negative space colored black.

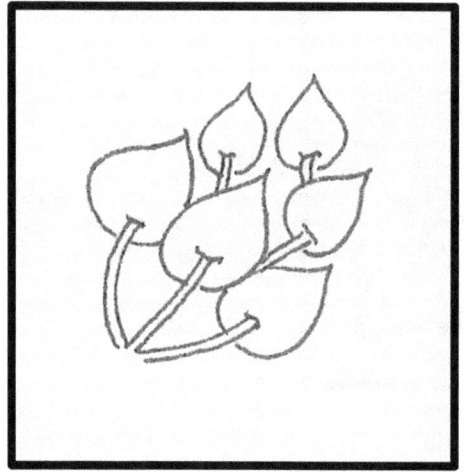

(1) Pokeleaf

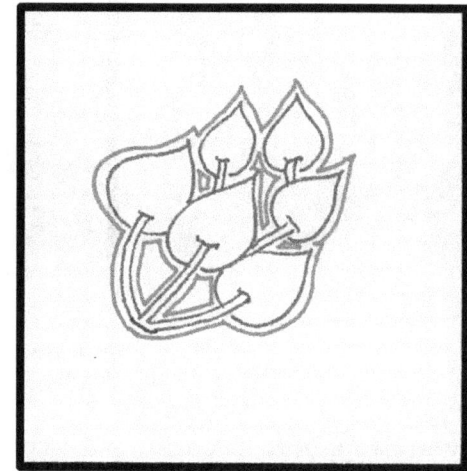

(2) Aura around Pokeleaf, including the space within the tangle

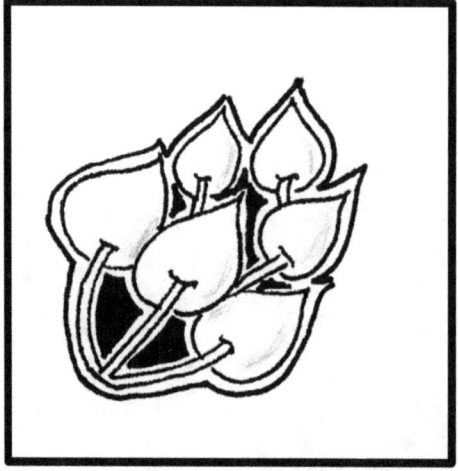

(3) Negative space within Pokeleaf colored black

In *Tip 8: Look ahead*, we saw that looking slightly ahead of the pen tip to where we wanted the pen to go resulted in smoother lines. You can apply that same principle to drawing auras to achieve a smoother, more even aura. Remember, you are not trying to do it "perfectly." (See *Tip 3: Don't worry about being perfect*)

When you can see the shape of the element you are **aura-ing,** it is easier to draw an even line. How you do this depends on whether you are left-handed or right- handed.

If you are left-handed, draw your auras on the left side of the element so your hand is not covering up the line you want to aura.

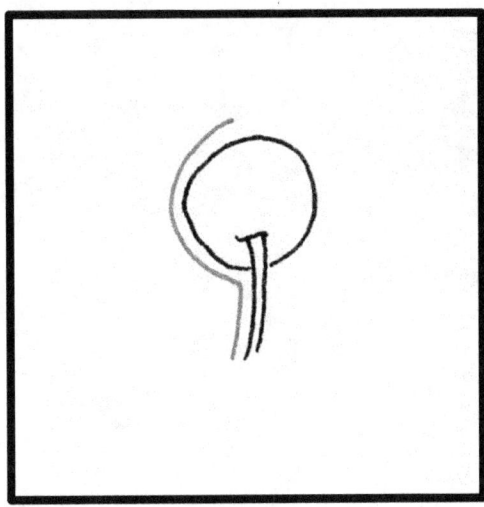

And for the same reason, if you are right-handed, draw your auras on the right side of the element.

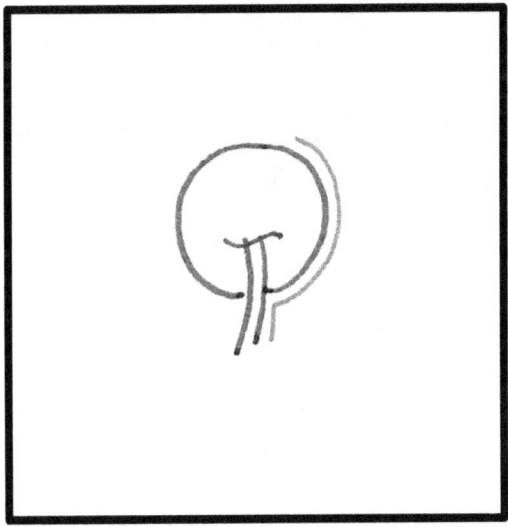

Keep turning your tile so that you can clearly see the line you want to aura. It is not necessary to draw the complete aura without lifting your pen. It is okay to draw part, lift your pen, turn your tile, and then continue.

You may find it helpful to imagine that the white space you create between the aura you are drawing and the tangle element is a small white line. Focusing on keeping the width of this white line consistent creates a more pleasing aura.

Tip 14: Circling around the orbs

When you draw a small **orb**, go back around it another time or two with your pen to make it more distinct. This subtle change strengthens and "cleans up" your smaller orbs. In the figure below, the orbs in the top row were drawn once, while those in the bottom row were drawn twice.

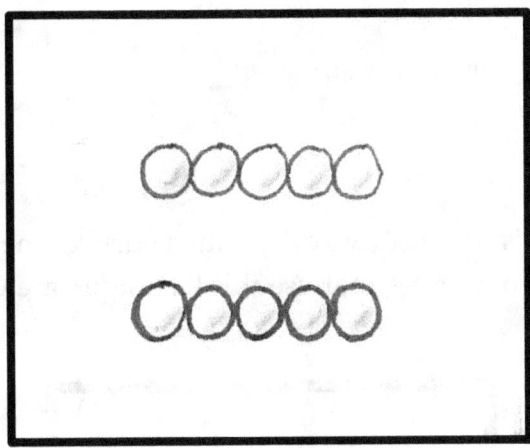

If you are drawing a small orb you can usually draw it without lifting your pen. Some people find it easier to draw large orbs by drawing one side, and then going back to the starting point, retracing a bit of the first arc and finishing it by drawing the other side, again retracing a bit of the first arc at the connection point.

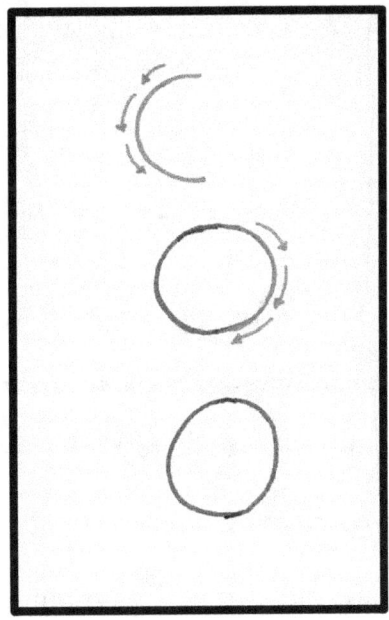

If you watch someone playing golf, tennis, or baseball you'll notice that they prepare to hit the ball, hit the ball, and then the club/racket/bat continues with a follow-through stroke.

A similar sequence can be used to create a smooth transition when you are joining orbs and lines. In Zentangle this is called "**Take Off and Land.**" The steps are:

1. *Prepare - take off,*
2. *Connect - draw the connecting stroke, and*
3. *Follow-through - land.*

To illustrate these steps let's connect two orbs with a curved line and then connect three orbs with a line. Examples of tangles that use this technique are Cadent, Crazy Huggins, and Well.

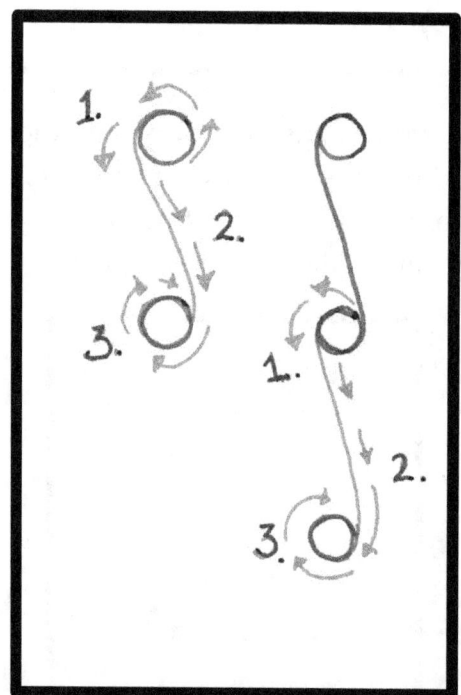

1. The *preparation* step traces around part of the top orb - "take off."

2. The *connecting* step draws the connecting line.

3. The *follow-through* step traces around part of the bottom orb - "land."

I use the "Take Off and Land" technique when I want a smooth transition from one element to another. Let's see what it looks like when connecting two lines with a curved line such as you would find in the tangles Drupe or Finery.

Figure one below demonstrates tracing a bit of the top line before drawing the curve. Figure two shows the curved line continuing and finishing by tracing a bit of the bottom line.

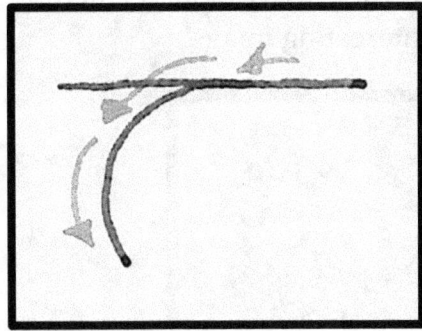

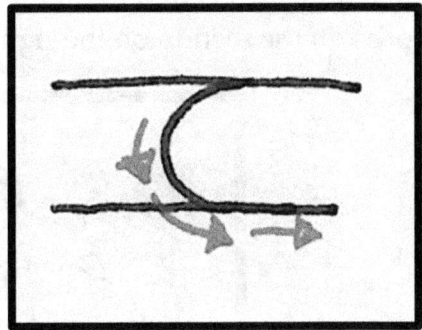

Figure 1   Figure 2

You can also use the words, "Take Off and Land" as a mantra when you are drawing elements or aura-ing. It may help slow you down and stay present with the stroke you are drawing.

Tip 15: Bigger may be better

When people begin working with Zentangle art they often draw their elements really small and close together, as if they are trying to squeeze as much onto a tile as possible. This can lead to uninteresting results that take longer to create than necessary.

The tile below shows the tangle "Tipple," drawn two ways. When you draw smaller elements more are needed to fill the space. Notice how the variety of large, medium, and small orbs on the section on the right creates a more interesting image.

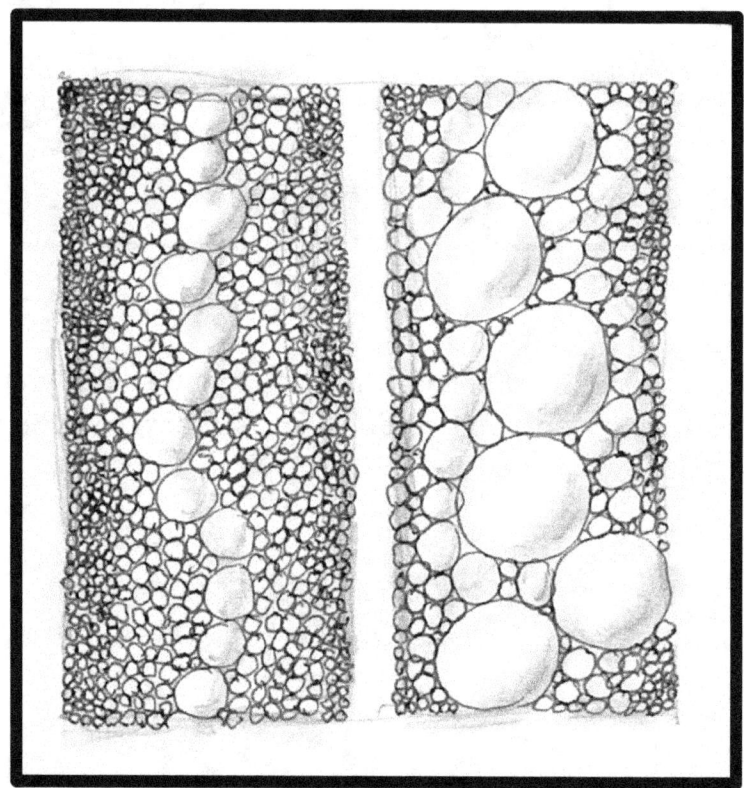

For some tangles making the shapes small can actually impede the flow of the pattern. One example is the tangle Tripoli, which is one of my favorites. If the triangles are small the inside pattern will be too tiny to be appreciated or there may not be enough room to add another pattern in the center.

The illustration below shows the tangle "Tripoli" using smaller triangles, medium triangles, and larger triangles.

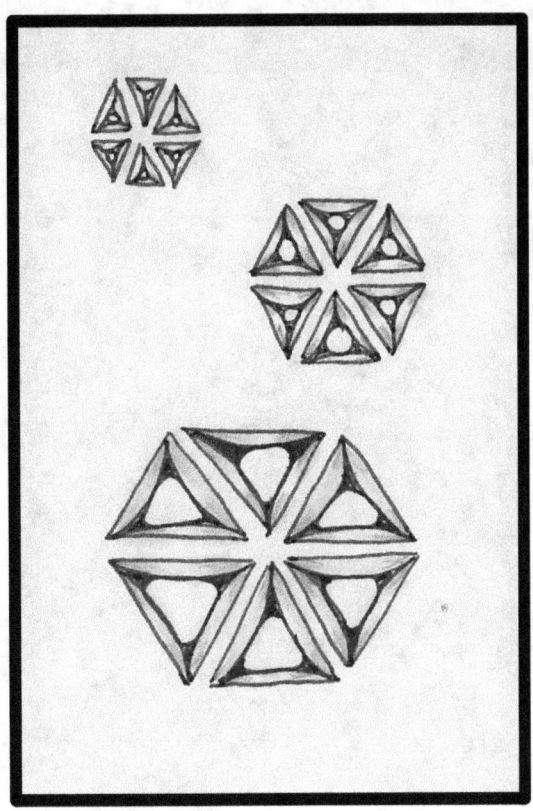

Do you have a specific tangle that you do not like right now? Could it be that you are working too small? Make your elements larger than you usually make them and see if that makes a difference for you.

Switching to a pen with a larger nib, such as a Micron 03, 05, or even an 08 pen, encourages you to draw larger because of the larger size. After using the larger-nibbed pen for awhile, try going back to your fine pointed pen, such as a Micron 01, and see if you are drawing elements larger now.

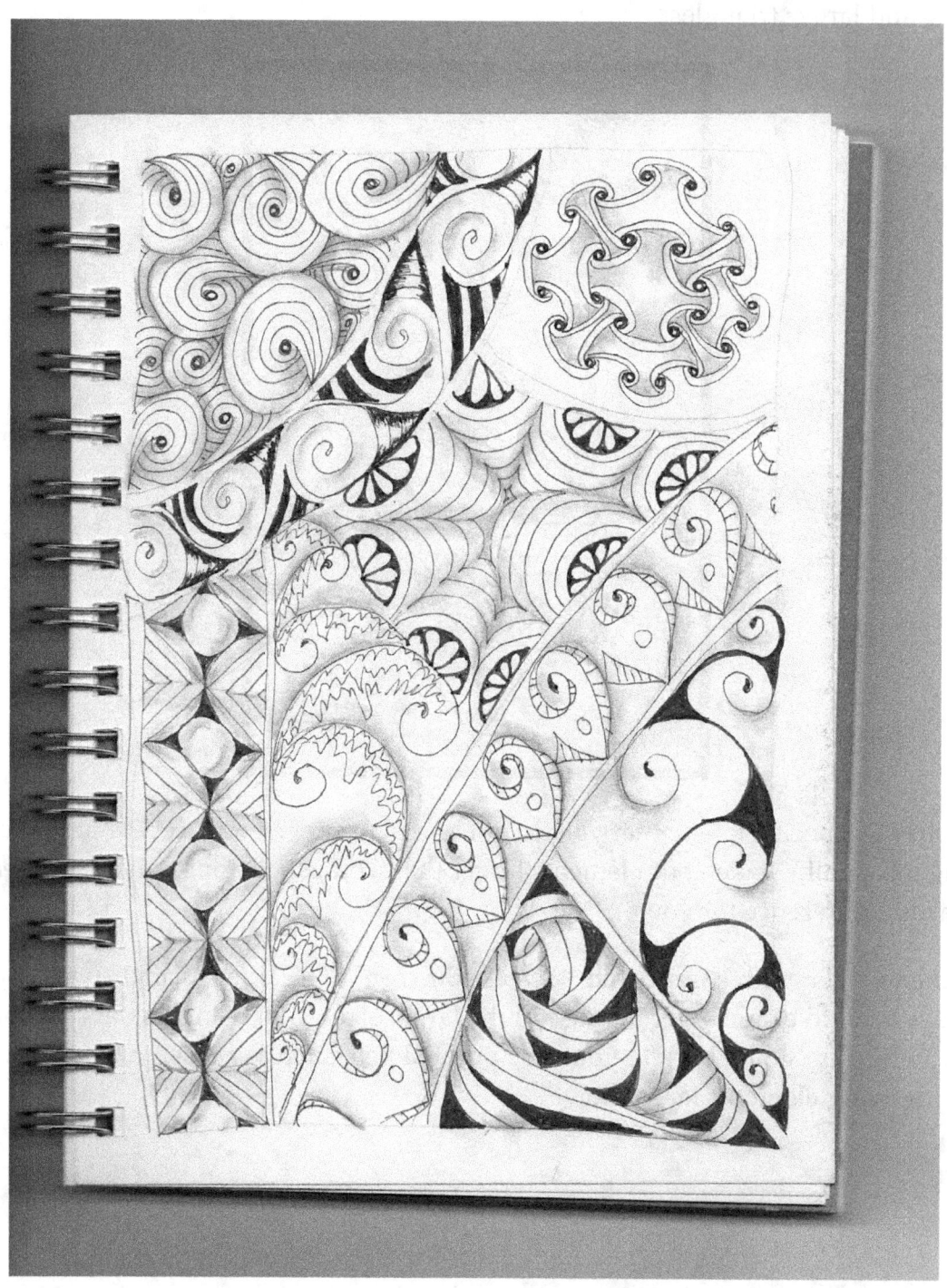

Chapter 4
Expand Your Tangling World

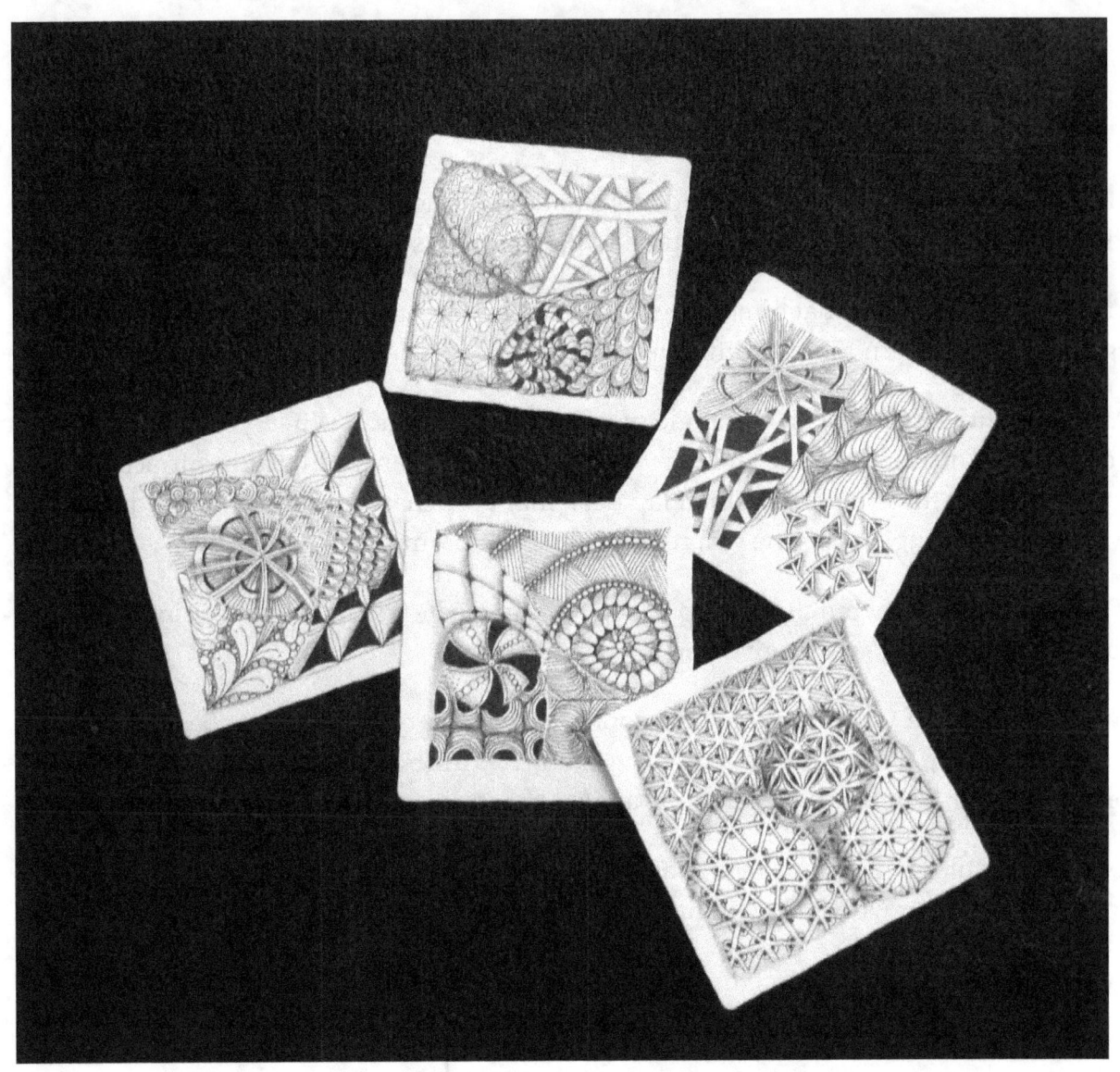

Tip 16: Look from a different angle

Moving away from something gives us a perspective that we miss when we are close to it. For example, when I visit my neighbor and look back at my house, it looks different.

One of my favorite movies is *Dead Poet's Society*. In one part of the movie, teacher John Keating encourages his students to look at life from a different angle.

> *"We must constantly look at things in a different way. Just when you think you know something you need to look at in a different way — even if it seems silly or wrong, you must try."*

He illustrates this by having the students stand on his desk and they see that the view is different. How many of us take the time to look at things from a different angle?

Take your tile and put it at arm's length or, even better, on a window ledge or lean it against a wall. Doesn't it look different?

Another "different angle" is the angle of your writing surface. When you are working, do you have your tile flat on the table? Try working with an angled writing surface to see if it works better for you. I use a small lap desk that I purchased online and I find that working on an angle eases the strain on my neck and arm.

If you do not wish to purchase a lap desk, you can create a similar effect using a 2" three-ringed binder positioned to give you an angled surface.

Another option, if you are sitting on a couch, easy chair, or sitting up in bed, is to use something solid, like a clip board, a piece of sturdy cardboard, etc. that you prop on a pillow or your bent knees to create the angled base.

Create your tiles with the surface at an angle and see if it feels different. Does the angled surface affect your work? Do you find less strain on your neck?

Tip 17: Tangle every day

You've probably heard the joke about the tourist in Manhattan who stopped renowned violinist Jascha Heifetz and asked, "Can you tell me how to get to Carnegie Hall?" Heifetz answered, "Yes! Practice, practice, practice."

With Zentangle art, as with all art forms, the way to improve is to do it every day. This is true if you are a musician, a dancer, a painter, a writer, an artist (yes, that is you!). The more you tangle, the better you get.

In his book, *The Outliers*, Malcolm Gladwell introduces us to the idea that we need 10,000 hours of dedicated and mindful practice to become a master of any subject. Whether you believe this to be true or not, I know from my own experience as a former musician, and now as a massage therapist and CZT, that the more I do, the better my work.

The word *practice* conjures up boring exercises and doing the same thing over and over. One of the definitions of the word *practice* is, "The actual application of a method, as opposed to theories about it." Instead of seeing it as practicing, think of it as mindful playing!

When you use the Zentangle Method on a regular basis, it becomes easier to focus, be present, relax, and create in a non-judgmental way. This daily application of gratitude and patience can have a profound impact on your ability to remain calm.

A student, who is a friend, remarked, "But I don't have time to tangle every day!" Knowing that she gives her son a back rub every night I suggested, "As you rub Noah's back why not do it in the shape of a tangle. I'm sure that he would LOVE to have you do Mooka or Flux on his back!" You don't always need to put pen to paper to practice your tangling. You can use a pencil, your whole arm in the air, a stick in the dirt...whatever tools you have.

One time a former student called to tell me that she fell and now her broken arm was in a cast. She said, "I'm so upset because I can't tangle to calm down." I suggested that she tangle with her non-dominant hand, which would not only give her the relaxation she is looking for, but also give her the opportunity to slow down and do each stroke mindfully. Knowing that this woman is a harsh judge of her own work, I suggested that she do it in a journal or sketchbook and view it as a tangling "exercise." Tangling in the journal also gave her space to do the stroke larger than she would on a 3½" square

Zentangle tile. Because of the limited movement due to the cast, the larger size would be easier to draw.

Another fun way to tangle each day is to purchase the "Tangle-a-Day calendar" created by CZT Carole Ohl (*http://openseedarts.blogspot.com/*). The calendar has space to tangle each day of the year. At the beginning of each month she shares a tile that she has created and shows the steps she took to create that tile.

I tangle one pattern (aka a **monotangle**) in the calendar each day. There are days when I do not like what I produce and others that surprise me. During a given week I include the tangle presented in the Square One Challenge and one of the tangles I use for the Diva Challenge. (*See Tip 19: Participate in a challenge and Appendix A for information about the Square One Challenge and the Diva Challenge.*)

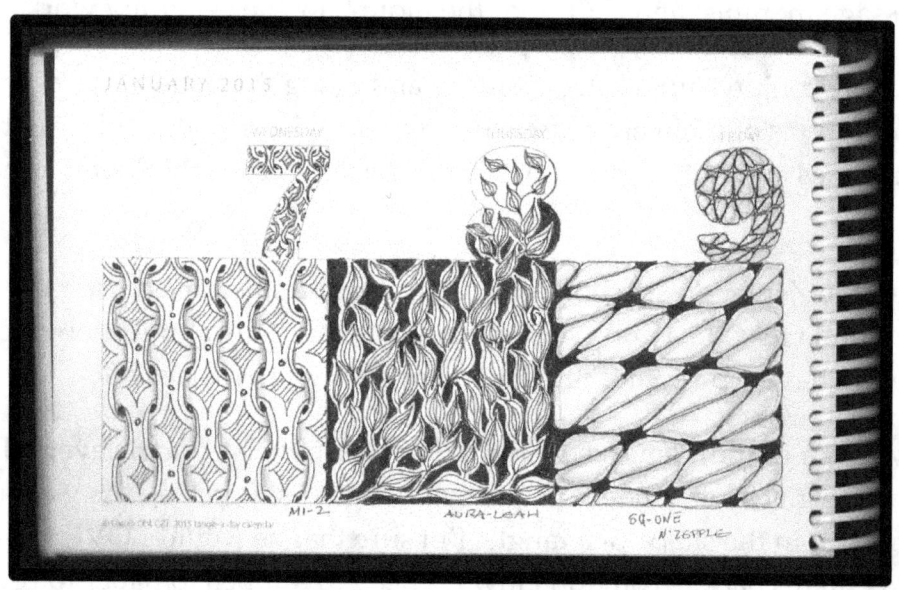

Drawing one tangle a day doesn't take a lot of time and you don't need to do a complete tile — only one *tangle*. Of course, the more you play with the tangles, the more practice you get. Many of us find that it is impossible to do only one tangle a day. Once we get started we don't want to stop. And some of us find it impossible to do just one *tile* a day for the same reason.

Tip 18: Use different size tiles

Are you using only one tile size?

Years ago I read a study that suggested that we should vary the height of the shoes we wear during any given week so that we use all of our leg muscles. When we wear shoes of the same height day after day, certain muscles will grow strong and others will become weaker because they aren't being used. I see a parallel with Zentangle art.

There are several sizes of the official tiles that have the Zentangle logo on the back. The original tile — the one that is considered to be the traditional Zentangle — is a 3½" square of creamy white Fabriano Tiepolo Printmaking paper.

There are also:

- 2" square tiles called Bijou tiles
- 10" square tiles called Opus tiles
- 4½" diameter round tiles, called **Zendalas**,
- 2½" x 3½" ATC (Artist Trading Card) tiles

To view the various options and color options, go to the official Zentangle website: *www.Zentangle.com.*

Of course, you can cut tiles of any size you want. When cutting your own tiles, it is advisable to use the best paper that you can afford. In all arts, the higher the quality of your tools, the easier it is to use the tools, and the better the results.

When I am not using the official 3½" square white tiles I prefer to cut my own from Mixed Media, Bristol (Vellum), or Stonehenge paper.

When the 10" Opus tiles first came out I worked on one in collaboration with another CZT. We were creating the tile as a birthday gift for a dear mutual friend. If it weren't for the collaboration I doubt that I would have ventured into the world of "Opus." That big square intimidated me and pushed me way out of my comfort zone, but because it was a collaborative effort I felt that I had to do my part. I found myself reluctant to start and became adept at procrastination. There was so much white space! I had to work larger than I ever had before and it was anxiety-producing. I clicked my black clogs (my version of ruby slippers) and repeated three times, *"There are no mistakes in Zentangle art."* Then I jumped in and just did it. When the tile was finished I was really glad that I had stepped beyond my barriers and worked on the Opus tile, which does't intimidate me anymore.

If you find yourself intimidated by a large tile you may want to find a buddy to work on the tile with you (to keep each other accountable) or find a CZT to help you and "just go for it."

Although I still gravitate toward the smaller tiles, I work larger every once in awhile to exercise that part of my muscle memory so it doesn't go dormant and to remind myself that it isn't intimidating once I put the first pen mark on the paper. The space is divided by the string and you do one part at a time. Yes, it takes more time than doing one smaller tile, but because you do not need to complete it in one setting that is not an issue. You complete it the same way you do your other Zentangle tiles: one stroke at a time.

Remember to exercise all parts of your muscle memory by using tiles of all different sizes — especially if they are out of your comfort zone. Larger, smaller, Zendala, ATC, or create your own sizes.

Tip 19: Participate in a challenge

I encourage you to participate in a challenge designed for tanglers — even if you never post your creation to the site and you are the only person to see your art. Creating a tile in response to a challenge is a great way to work with patterns that you haven't seen before, have been resisting, or have forgotten about. What will this do for you? I find that the challenges gently push me to go beyond what is comfortable and by the time I finish my tile (or usually tiles) my discomfort is left behind. It stretches my abilities, sharpens my skills, and expands my creativity beyond what I think is possible.

For example, one of the Diva Challenges was to use the official Zentangle pattern named *Diva Dance*. I had tried this pattern before doing the challenge and didn't like it at all. It was never going to be high on my list of "do again" tangles.

I was tempted to skip the challenge and then thought, *"Duh! What do you think challenge means? Are you really only going to do those that you find to be 'easy' and skip those that 'challenge' you? Kinda defeats the purpose of doing the tiles, right?"* I took up the challenge and guess what! I loved doing this tangle and have added it to my list of favorites.

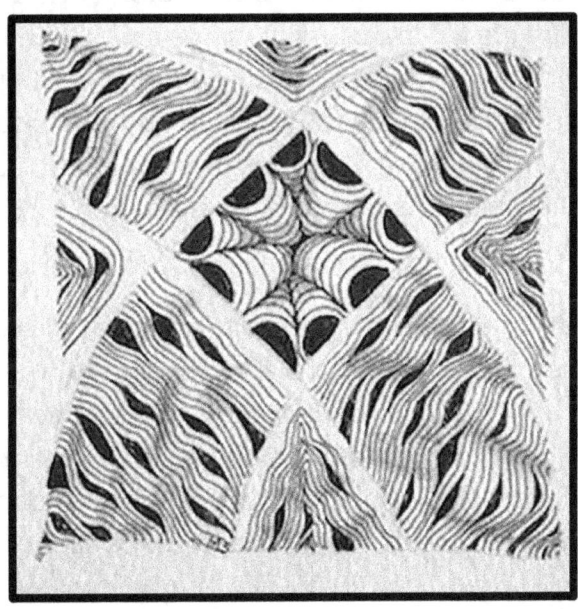

This was my tile in response to the Diva Challenge.

When you view the tiles that others have created in response to the challenge you may see a tangle that speaks to you, or a tangleation that you never thought to use. I have seen two or three tangles used together in a way that piques my interest. I find participating in these challenges and viewing how other people respond to each challenge to be interesting, encouraging, and educational.

There are many online weekly challenges for tanglers. Some are websites and some are Facebook pages. Find one that feels like a fit for you and challenge yourself each week. My favorites are The *Diva Challenge* and *Square One: Purely Zentangle®*.

The *Diva Challenge* (*www.iamthediva.blogspot.com*), created by Canadian CZT Laura Harms, is posted Mondays, unless it is a Canadian holiday, in which case it is posted on Tuesday. The first Monday of each month is usually a UMT (Use My Tangle) challenge. People submit a link to the step-outs for their tangles and Laura randomly selects one for that week's challenge. It is a great way to play with tangles that may be new to you. All of the challenges encourage and inspire us to expand our awareness and creativity.

My other favorite is technically not considered a challenge. It is the Facebook group, *Square One: Purely Zentangle®*. Each Friday Administrator Chris Titus CZT posts the name and step-outs for a tangle for members to create a tile, with the tangle as their focus, using only a 3½" square white tile, with black ink, and a graphite pencil. No other size, no other color. The purpose is to get us back to basics and it is amazing to see what people post. Looking at the black on white keeps us from being distracted by color. It shows us all of the incredible beauty that can be created with a pen, a piece of paper, and a pencil.

For some, the black ink on a white Zentangle tile is limiting but that is a good reason to do it. You may be surprise yourself, especially if you are used to working with color. You might find that the relaxed focus of the Zentangle Method comes more easily when you go back to the traditional black and white. If you are not online, find a tangle buddy or a group to tangle with on a regular basis. I know of one group that meets once a week to work on their calendars and they challenge and encourage each other while having fun.

Tip 20: Create tangleations

Are you a pattern collector? Have you scoured *Tanglepatterns.com*, *Pinterest*, or other sites that feature tangles and have you printed pages and pages of tangle step-outs? Do you get excited every time you read about a new way to organize your patterns? Do you spend hours maintaining your tangle collection? Do you spend your precious tangle time searching your collection for the "perfect" tangle? If so, you are one of many who are pattern collectors. I think that we are probably all pattern collectors when we begin to explore the world of tangling. There are so many intriguing tangles out there!

As a new tangler, I remember thinking, "I need to know a lot of tangles so I can spontaneously choose my next pattern. If I only know a few tangles won't I become bored? Won't my tiles all look the same? I'd better learn a lot of patterns." Yes, I was a pattern collector. I soon realized that although I printed the step-outs for lots of patterns, I was still using my four or five favorite tangles and became very comfortable with them. These comfortable tangles are called "Mac and Cheese" tangles.

Do we really need a whole lot of different tangles? What if we were to explore our familiar tangles and change them so we are looking at the patterns in a different way? When you change a tangle it is called a tangleation.

In their book, *Pattern Play*, Cris Letourneau and Sonya Yencer invite you to do just that — explore tangles. This wonderful reference book offers information on how tangleations can expand your repertoire. I learned that it is better to fully explore a few patterns that I like and am comfortable using than to dabble with lots of patterns that keep me from focusing on the quality of my strokes.

I gravitate toward **grid tangles**. However, I like to see play with tangle to see what happens if I change a pattern from its original format to something unique. I like to take the grid tangle and experiment with it to see if it can become an organic pattern. Or take the organic pattern and see what it would look like in a grid.

Playing with the tangles helps me to look at patterns in a different way. I am not always successful in morphing the pattern, but I always learn something. When it is successful I have more ways to use the pattern. So, take your favorite tangles and see what you can do with them.

Shown below is a page from one of my sketch books showing how I played with my tangle, Orb Pods, and tangleations. It shows the pattern as an organic tangle, as a grid pattern, different backgrounds and different configurations. You may also notice that I was playing with what to call this pattern. You can see the step- outs for Orb Pods on my website: *www.taooftangling.com*, click on the *Patterns* tab and select *Orb Pods*.

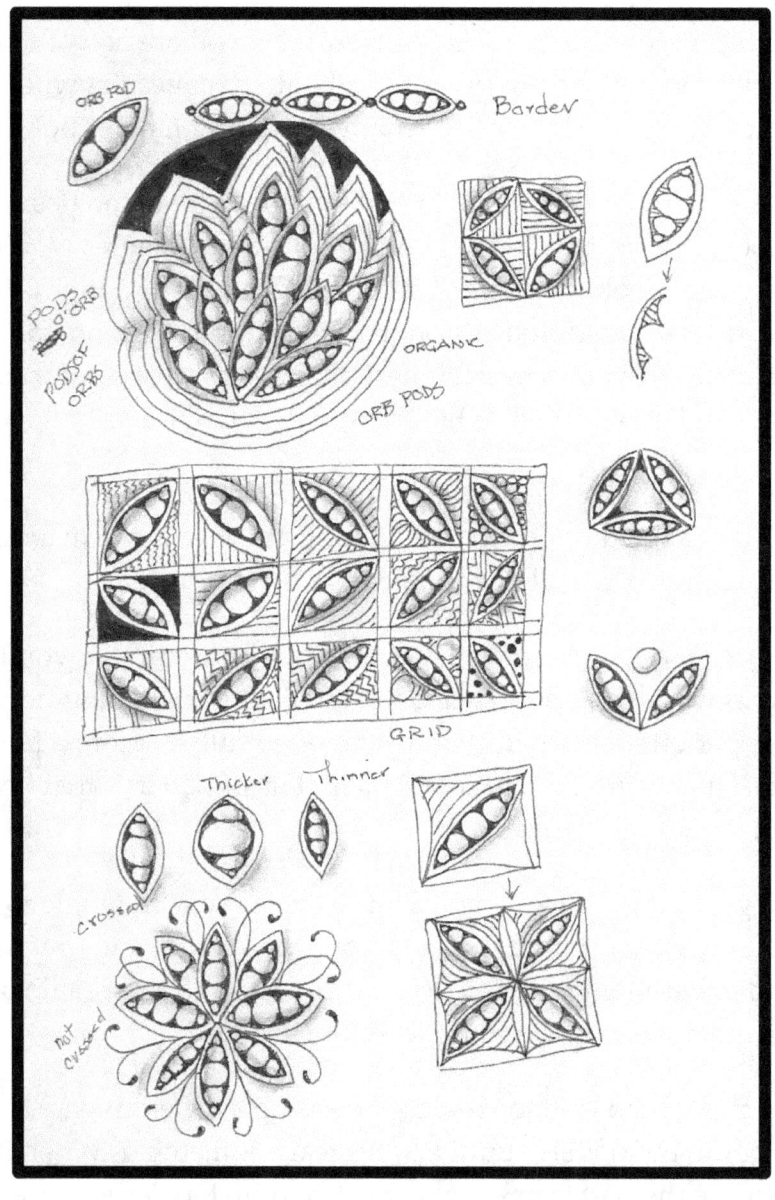

Chapter 5
Play, Play, Play

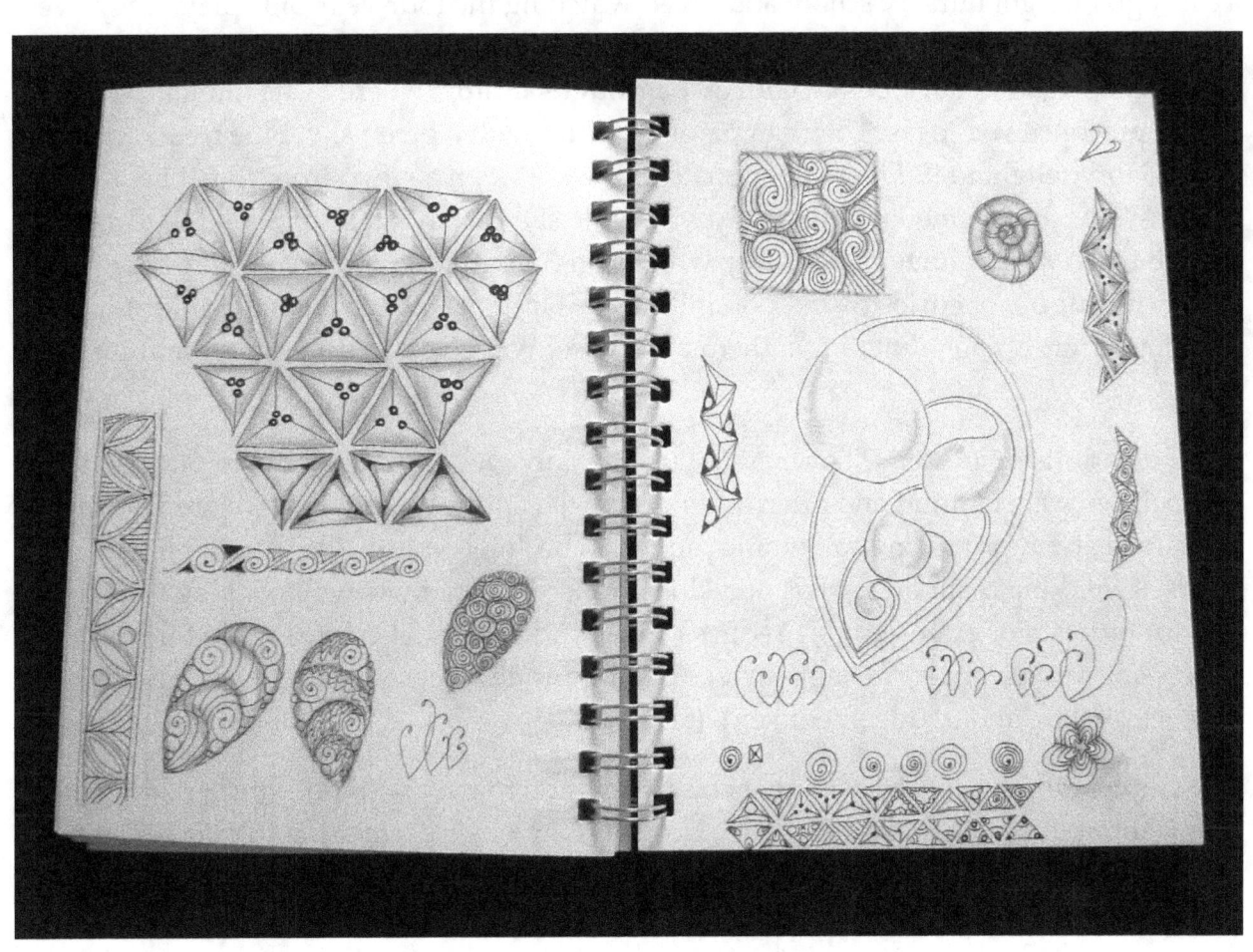

Tip 21: Give yourself permission to play

Play energizes us and enlivens us. It eases our burdens. It renews our natural sense of optimism and opens us up to new possibilities.

— Stuart Brown, MD, contemporary American psychiatrist

Years ago I taught nursery school and loved watching the four-year-olds play. They live fully in the moment. If they have a disagreement with a friend, ten minutes later they are best friends again. They operate with a **"beginner's mind,"** where everything is new and free of preconceived ideas. They can paint a picture with a green sky, blue trees, and red grass... and delight in it. I remember one child who put on a gown from the "Play Clothes" box and teamed it with a hard hat while she pretended to cook on the toy stove. They have *wonderful* imaginations, say what is on their minds, and are an endless, delightful supply of curiosity and possibilities — without conclusion and without judgement, unless an adult taught them otherwise. We have a lot to learn from four-year-olds.

What do adults do for play? For many of us, the only way we know how to play is in a competitive state of mind and often as an organized sport. We feel that we are wasting time if we aren't producing something judged to be "meaningful." When you find yourself thinking that playing has no value, think of the many benefits of play for you and for others. For example, play reduces stress and anxiety; it creates space for self-expression and creativity to happen; it offers time and support to experiment and to practice skills without judgement; and, it is fun!

Are you waiting for someone to give you permission to play with no expected outcome? Think about those four-year-olds. They don't ask anyone's permission to play. Imagine what life would be like if we could be that joyful again. Play for the sake of playing, for all the reasons it is beneficial. If you *are* waiting for someone to give you permission, be that person. Give *yourself* permission right now! If you have trouble giving yourself permission, then know that you certainly have my permission to play!

How do you know if you are playing while you are tangling? If you are more interested in the *process* of creating the strokes than in *creating* a tile, you are playing. If you are using your pens and other art tools for enjoyment rather than a serious or practical purpose, you are playing.

If this is a new concept for you, schedule a time to play. What if you made a weekly "play date" with yourself? You might decide to go to a favorite place in nature or find a quiet spot at home. When my children were young, I would find time to retreat to either the local university library or the town library. It was quiet and free from distractions.

One of the benefits of Zentangle art is that it is portable. If there is a place to put your tile you can tangle.

Play time is important, not only to let your creative juices run, but also to balance the constant hamster wheel many of us call life with down time, relaxation, and fun.

Tip 22: Keep a "Play Book"

I have several sketchbooks of different sizes. You may already have a portable sketchbook or journal that you tuck into a pocket or purse so you can spontaneously jot down ideas, sketches, inspirational thoughts, etc.

This tip is about a large sketchbook that is not meant to be portable. I recommend a book that is a minimum of 8½ by 11 inches. Instead of seeing it as a "workbook" designate it as a "Play Book" and use it with the same carefree attitude as the four-year-olds playing in nursery school. Use this book to play with your writing tools and ideas, musings, or whatever suits your fancy. If you are comfortable journaling, add some words about your work, your state of mind, or what you discovered while you were playing.

The quality of the paper in your Play Book dictates which tools you can use. For my Play Books, I buy relatively inexpensive sketchbooks. The quality of the paper is not thick enough to use juicy watercolor paints, but I can use colored pencils. Most of the time I draw the tangle elements with a black fine point gel pen and shade with a graphite pencil. I use colored pencils when I want to explore which colors, when put together, are pleasing to my eyes, or to see what happens when I blend two different colored pencils, adding notes for future reference.

This book is like a private sandbox or playhouse where you are free to create and experiment. It is a good idea to keep the contents of this book private and not share what you create with anyone. If I happen to create something that I really like and want to share with others I replicate it, as closely as possible, on a tile or in one of my other sketchbooks so that my Play Book is still private.

Why do we work differently when we know that others are going to see a page from our book? We have a fear of being judged.

By keeping the contents private, we keep the judgements of others, *and of ourself,* at bay. The freedom from judgment allows us to plant the seeds of new ideas and awarenesses. Think of the art on these pages as simply marks on a page. There may be patterns on top of patterns. I often put tangles between the strings formed by the scribbles and add shading. This image is a close replication of artwork from my Play Book.

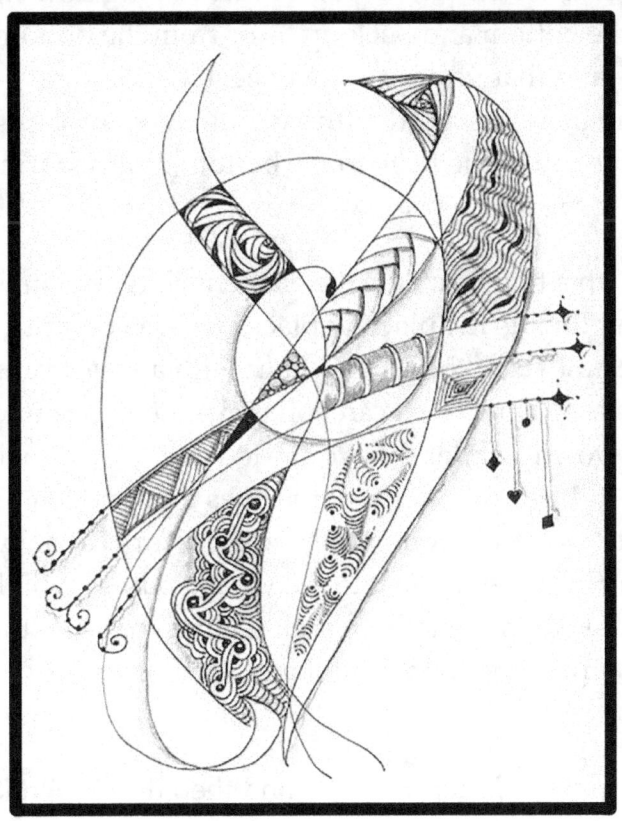

The Play Book is a place where the marks you make do not need to make sense. I use the book to expand my imagination and to live like a four-year-old again. This book gives me a chance to play with lines, forms, ideas, motifs, and processes. This is where I practice tangles that I find challenging, see what tangleations I can come up with, or warm up before I do a tile. It helps to calm the internal critic that would like to turn me against my belief that I am an artist and creative. In this book I can scribble, let loose, screw things up — sometimes on purpose — or whatever I feel like doing in that moment. I can draw like a child with a temper tantrum on one page, flip the page, and create graceful spirals with mindful strokes — from the top of the page to the bottom and one on top of the other. I am free to color the sky green and the grass purple, if that's what I want in that moment, and no one is going to try to figure out what that means or suggest that I see a therapist.

In the Play Book you have a large amount of space to fill so use the whole page. One of the benefits of the size of the Play Book is that it allows you to draw large elements using your whole arm, not just your wrist. When we draw long lines using our whole arm they are graceful and flowing.

Let your lines and patterns fill the whole page. Practice long flowing lines that go from the top of the page to the bottom and back up — or from the bottom of the page to the top and back down. Draw lines that go across the page, too. I did one page to see how evenly spaced I could draw my lines. It started with medium long strokes going up and down and then I went from the top of the page to the bottom. Pretty boring to look at, right? But no one else is going to see it, and it was a great exercise for me.

If you are struggling with a tangle, create the elements larger than you ever did before. Making it large often highlights the place or places where you are getting "stuck." How big can you draw the elements of the tangle? Start with a *huge* triangle and create a page of the official tangle Tripoli. How large can you make the first rounded end stroke of the official tangle Mooka? Does it matter that your Mooka looks more like Mocha? Throw caution to the wind — it doesn't matter that the lines don't match up. Actually, it is more fun when lines are really wonky. (Don't you love that word "wonky"?) Sometimes I make the lines anything but straight, just to see what a pattern will look like. There is a freedom in creating crooked lines and then seeing what comes of the pattern. Sometimes it resembles what I have pictured in my mind and sometimes it doesn't. That's fine! I just flip the page.

Try asking yourself, *"What would happen if...?"* and then do it. "What would happen if I used only curvy lines instead of straight lines?" or "What would happen if I used colored pencil lines for a string?" or "What happens if I use straight lines to do Purk?" Like the results? Great. Don't like the results? Great. Just go on to the next page.

I find that, after playing in this book, when I go back to the smaller Zentangle tile the tangles flow much more easily.

Chapter 6
Time for Appreciation

Tip 23: Practice gratitude

Enjoy the process of drawing tangles and at the end of the day remember to take a few moments to be grateful for whatever you created. Really appreciate all that you did, even if it is only one tangle; all that you learned; and all the fun and enjoyment you had creating your artwork. This is a part of the Zentangle method that is easy to overlook. If you practice being grateful each day, it becomes automatic and very satisfying.

Would you be willing to show gratitude for all the wonderful discoveries while creating a tile or playing in your Play Book? Would you be willing to express gratitude for those strokes and tiles that do not meet your standards? They teach us a lot! To paraphrase a quote I read many years ago, we find comfort among the tiles we find pleasing to our eyes and growth among those that we don't.

In her book, *Simple Abundance*, author Sarah Ban Breathnach shares information on, as she states, *"how your daily life can be an expression of your authentic self."* She suggests different tools to achieve this. One of the tools is to keep a gratitude journal. Every night, in a journal or in your Play Book, you write down five things you are grateful for that day. The next night you write five different things to be grateful for, never repeating yourself. The idea is to come from a place where we can be grateful for what we have and to raise our awareness to those moments of the day rather than focusing on what we think we are lacking. The things you are grateful for do not need to be dramatic or earth shaking. They can be as simple as "I saw a strong, independent flower growing between the cracks in my driveway," "Drawing the tangle Paradox was effortless today,"or "I got in the elevator and a woman gave me an angelic smile."

When talking about keeping a gratitude journal, I often share an entry from one of my own journals. It was the day I was running late for work and a glass tumbler fell from the dish drainer, hit the counter, and bounced on the floor...but did not break. I was so grateful that I didn't need to take time, which I didn't really have, to clean it up before I quickly headed out the door. How does it get any better than that?

Tip 24: Just say, "Thank you!"

How many of us allow the judgments of others to determine how we feel about our tiles or artwork? We don't trust that if it is worthy in our eyes it doesn't matter what others think. In my Play Book I choose to see *everything* as worthy and ask myself, "Is this a '*do again*' or a '*don't do again*'?" No judgement, just a choice. Sometimes when I look at it again later, my "don't do again" strokes become "do again" strokes.

What happens when we hear something positive about our work? Do we immediately dismiss it? How many of us feel that we don't deserve it? How many of us compare ourselves to other Zentangle artists and find our work lacking? How many of us have a difficult time seeing ourselves as artists? How many of us have difficulty accepting the simplest of compliments?

A wise calligraphy friend said, *"When someone gives you a compliment, don't defend for or against it, just say 'Thank You!' and no more."* It took awhile before I could just say "Thank you" and no more. I would go into explanations such as: "Thank you. I'm sure I can do better next time. I don't really like the way my Mooka came out." Sound familiar? Now it is an automatic response for me to simply say "Thank you!" and stop there. The next time someone pays you a compliment — whether it is related to your artwork or not — try saying "Thank you!" Period.

Tip 25: Appreciate where you are

I want to leave you with one last thought. One of the greatest challenges to our creativity is comparing our art work to that of others. No matter what you perceive to be your level of skill with Zentangle art, appreciate where you are.

To illustrate this I want to share an experience I had as a calligrapher. I had been doing calligraphy for about six months and decided to go to the International Calligraphy Convention with a group from our calligraphy guild. This conference was a week of taking classes from teachers who were recognized for their contributions to the field of calligraphy and revered by calligraphers around the world. At this convention the instructors took classes right along with the students. You could tell which were instructors because they had ribbons attached to their name badges.

For my first class, "Calligraphy and the Fine Arts," we had been told to bring a fine art medium to the class. I brought a set of inexpensive pan watercolors.

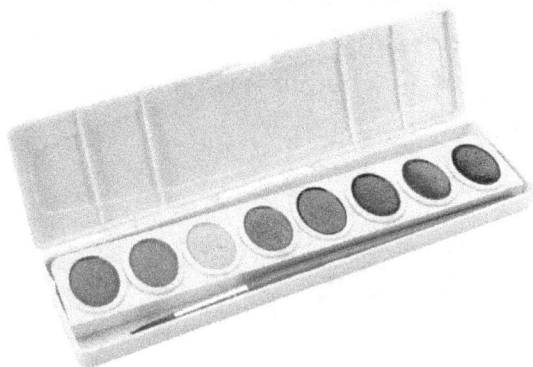

When I walked into the room there were twelve students, most of them with ribbons on their badges. Fortunately, I sat in the back row between two instructors, Nancy and Bonnie.

As I sat there, I suddenly realized how foolish and naive I was. It had never occurred to me that I needed to bring paper, ink, and pens. I just brought my pan of watercolor paints. Nancy gave me paper, Bonnie let me use one of her pens.

The instructor, Alan, an amazing calligrapher and man, had studied Zen Buddhism. After a short meditation he gave us a quote by Ashleigh Brilliant: "I hope I get what I want before I stop wanting it." He had us write the words from the bottom of the paper to the top, being aware that the pen would land where it was supposed to, so there were no mistakes (sound familiar?).

I wrote with childlike letters and put a big red stop sign in the middle. I looked over and Nancy was doing her piece using a beautiful lettering called Neuland and Bonnie used an equally beautiful pointed pen script lettering. I quietly slipped my work behind me and went on to the next exercise.

One of the people in the class, who has works hanging in museums, said, "Bring your work into the hallway and I will critique it." I thought, "What? Really? Judge my piece compared to the beautiful lettering around me? I don't think so!" So I went down the hall without my work.

As the students were putting their artwork on the floor to be critiqued, Alan looked them over and noticed that my piece was not there. He said, "I don't see the stop sign. I want the person who did the stop sign to get their work and put it in the hall." I sheepishly went back to the room and got the piece. As I walked back to the hallway I prayed that it wouldn't be critiqued and it wasn't.

Four days later I ran into Alan. He pointed at me and said, "You! I have been looking all over for you. Do you still have the piece with the stop sign?" When I said that I did, he continued, "Promise me that you will frame it. Your piece is so corny it is wonderful! My only regret is that I didn't think of it first." Wow! Imagine my surprise! All those ribboned people in the room and he saw something in my piece of art and liked it!

Looking at the piece from a different perspective only time could provide, I realized that while my technical skills weren't even close to those of Bonnie and Nancy, the piece has a naive quality and was produced with a beginner 's mind. I was open to possibilities that those who were more experienced wouldn't even entertain. It had worthiness that I did not see because I compared my work to those around me and felt inadequate. I ignored the fact that I was new to this art form and instead expected my work to match the technical quality of work from those who had been doing it for years. With this comparison I concluded that my work fell short. It took someone else to see the beauty in this simple piece of art.

I tell this story to show that you also have something to cherish and contribute, no matter where you feel you fall on the skill level continuum. Remember to use your beginner 's mind where there is no judgement.

I encourage you to to be inspired by those whose work you admire and to resist the temptation to compare your work to that of those you believe to be more creative, artistic, talented, etc. You have qualities that only you possess. You are one of the people whose badge doesn't need a ribbon and you are capable of creating something unique and quite extraordinary.

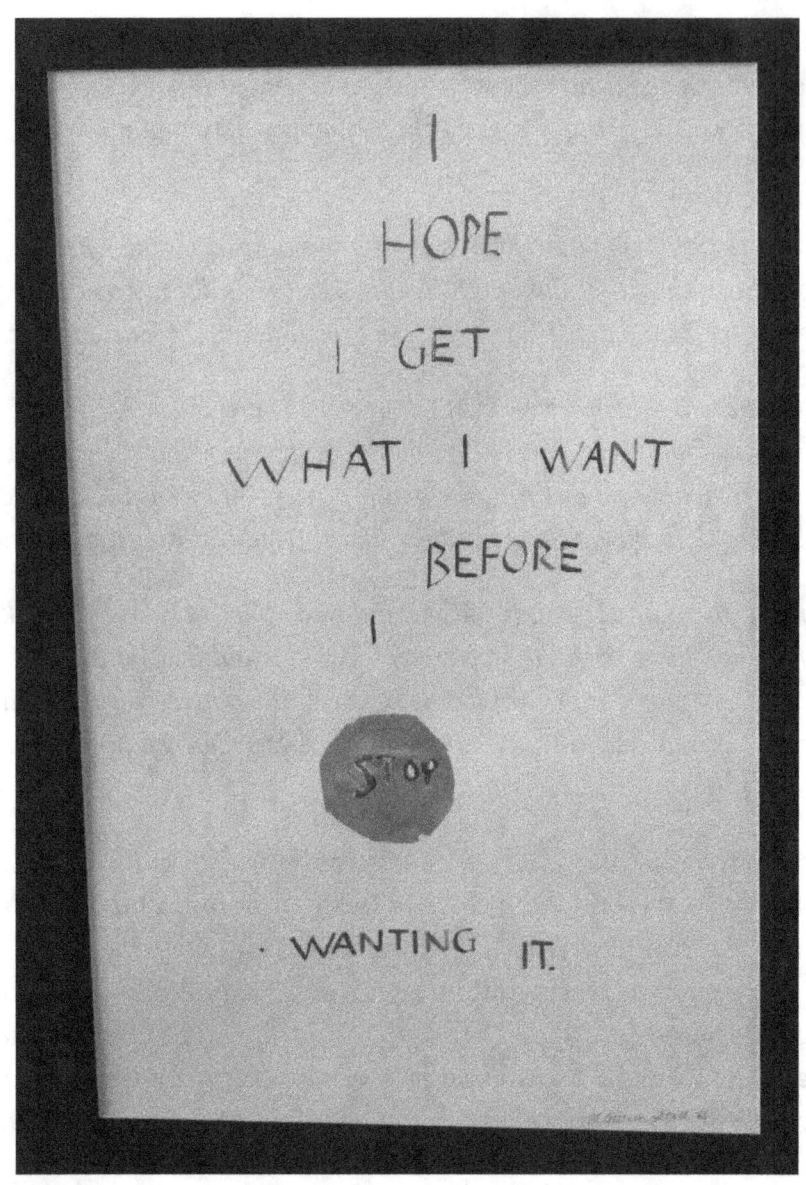

So, dear readers, it is my hope that you have found at least one new idea, suggestion, or tip that you can embrace so that you are tangling smarter, not harder. And now... it's time to tangle!

Glossary

Archival

Archival means that the ink or paper is chemically stable and will last a lifetime, given proper care. Paper that is not archival turns yellow as it ages and deteriorates. Sometimes this happens in a relatively short time span and sometimes it takes years. If you use pens that are not archival the colors may change over time.

Aura

To aura a line or shape it means to draw a line parallel to an existing line in order to outline a pattern or area. *For more about auras, refer to "Tip 13: Aura-ing around the tangle."*

Aura-ing

The act of drawing auras around a tangle or around the elements, thus creating negative spaces.

Beginner's Mind

This Zen Buddhist phrase refers to being open to all possibilities with little or no preconceived notion of what something should be, look like, or have. When we learn something new we approach the subject with an enthusiastic attitude and want more.

Certified Zentangle Teacher

This is someone who has taken the Certified Zentangle Teacher ™ Seminar and is certified by the founders of the Zentangle Method, Rick Roberts and Maria Thomas, to teach their method of creating Zentangle art.

CZT™

Acronym for Certified Zentangle Teacher. Only CZTs are authorized to teach the Zentangle Method.

Grid Tangle

This is a pattern that is based on a series of vertical and horizontal parallel lines that forms the base structure of the tangle. Examples of official Zentangle grid patterns include Bales, Knightsbridge, Huggins, Cubine, etc.

Mac and Cheese Tangles

As we learn different tangles there are a few that we really like and use over and over. Because we find them to be comfortable and satisfying, we call them our Mac and Cheese tangles.

Monkey Mind

This is a Buddhist phrase that refers to the times when our minds are distracted and jump from thought to thought like a monkey jumping from tree to tree.

Monotangle

Coined by CZT Laura Harms, a monotangle is a tile that contains only one tangle or one tangle and some tangleations of that tangle.

Muscle Memory

As you repeatedly practice a particular movement with frequency, you build new pathways in your brain so it can reproduce the movement without conscious thought.

Negative Space

This is the open space between elements, parts of elements, or around the tangle. Refer to *"Tip 13: Aura-ing around the tangle"* for an illustration of negative space.

Nib

The tip of a pen.

Official Zentangle Tangles

These are tangles created by Zentangle, Inc. Some of the official tangles have not been published, which means that the step-outs for them are available only to CZTs. To learn these unpublished tangles you need to take a class with a CZT.

Orb

We use the word "orb" instead of the word "circle." To many, the word "circle" means that the artist is drawing as close to a perfectly round shape as possible. An orb can be circular without the pressure of it having to be perfectly round.

Organic Tangles

These are patterns that "grow" as you draw them. They do not have an underlying structure such as a grid. Examples of organic patterns include official Zentangle tangles Mooka, Zinger, Flux, and Pokeroot.

Step-outs
Instructions that show, step by step, how to create a tangle with the new strokes in red ink.

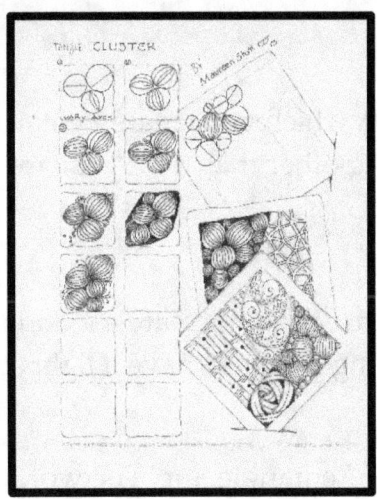

String
A random line, drawn in pencil, that divides a tile into sections in which you draw your tangles.

Take Off and Land
A term coined by the founders of the Zentangle Method to describe the process to create smooth line transitions between two Zentangle elements You begin by tracing the first element *(take off)*, drawing the connecting stroke, and end the connecting strokes by tracing a bit of the next element *(and land)*. *(Refer to Tip:14: Circling around the orbs)*

Tangle
A named pattern that has been broken down into simple, repeated strokes composed of a combination of one or more tangle elements. In its verb form "tangle" means to draw a tangle. You tangle a tangle, and in that process create Zentangle art. You don't *"Zentangle"* your tile, you *tangle* your tile. Tangles are non-representational, use only tangle elements, and can be taught.

Tangle Elements
The elements of a tangle are: a line, a dot, a curved line, a wavy "S," and an orb. Tangles are made up of one or more of these elements.

Tangleation

In music this is called a variation on a theme. In Zentangle, you take a tangle and alter it, change its proportions, change one element, etc., all the while keeping the "bones" of the tangle intact.

Tile

This is what we call the paper on which you create Zentangle art or Zentangle Inspired Art (ZIA). When we use anything other than a 3½" square white tile, the artwork is considered ZIA.

Zendala®

These 4⅝" diameter round tiles are used to create a mandala using Zentangle Art. They come plain or pre-strung, meaning that they have a light string printed on them.

Zentangle®

This is a registered trademark of Zentangle, Inc. The word **Zentangle** should be used as an ***adjective, not a verb***. For example: Zentangle art or Zentangle Method. The word "Zentangle" is often misused, especially by authors and those on videos who have not been trained in this method. If you are creating Zentangle art, you are "tangling." For more information about the legal use of the term, please go to the official Zentangle website: *www.Zentangle.com*.

Zentangle® Art

To be considered Zentangle Art a piece of work needs to be created on an official Zentangle white 3½" square tile, using black ink plus graphite pencil for shading. All other art is considered Zentangle Inspired Art or ZIA.

Zentangle® Method

The Zentangle Method, created by Rick Roberts and Maria Thomas, is a relaxing, fun way to create beautiful images using structured patterns. This method of creating Zentangle art can only be taught by a Certified Zentangle Teacher (CZT).

Zentangle Inspired Art

Any artwork that uses materials other than the official white 3½" square tiles with black ink and graphite shading. Artwork created using more than the basic tools or other tools is considered ZIA. If you tangle on fabric, wood, metal, ceramics, glass, etc. it is considered ZIA. Likewise, if you add color, it is also considered ZIA.

ZIA

Acronym for Zentangle Inspired Art.

APPENDIX A

Recommendations for resources and tools

This list is not meant to be inclusive. These are resources and tools that I use and recommend.

1. Books:

Joy of Zentangle by Marie Browning and Suzanne McNeill
Made in the Shade by Cris Letourneau
One Zentangle A Day by Beckah Krahula
Pattern Play by Cris Letourneau and Sonya Yencer

2. Music I listen to while tangling:

Canyon Trilogy by R. Carlos Nakai
Healing Chakras by David Young
The Healing Flute by Werner John
Renaissance by David Young
Almost any music by Windham Hill

Music on Pandora radio stations. I use the shuffle option so the music from each station is randomly selected. The stations that I like to listen to include:

> Baby Mozart Radio
> Baroque Radio
> Meditation Music Radio
> Musical Spa Radio
> Native American Flute Radio

3. Websites and Blogs:

The Tao Of Tangling: *www.TaoOfTangling.com*

> This is my website. Here you can view my blog, which includes tiles that I submit to the Diva Challenge (see below). You can also view and register for my upcoming classes and events. The "Patterns" tab shows the step-outs for tangles that I have created.

On my home page you can sign up for my free online newsletter that is published four times a year. If you have a question or would like to suggest a topic about Zentangle art to be discussed in the newsletter, feel free to contact me and share your ideas.

The Diva Challenge: *www.iamthedivaczt.blogspot.com*

This is a weekly challenge posted on Mondays unless it is a Canadian holiday, in which case the challenge is posted on Tuesday. Even if you do not submit your tiles, you can learn a lot by looking at the tiles that others submit as their answer to the challenge. When you get to the site you will see a list of names. These are the individuals who submitted a tile. Click on the person's name to see their tile. The tiles are usually posted on the artist's blog page. Those who do not have a blog post their tiles on Flickr, Pinterest, or Instagram. I find it educational and helpful to read some, if not all, of the comments posted on the blog pages. Looking at the various interpretations of the challenge is both inspirational and encouraging.

Square One: Purely Zentangle Group: A Facebook group

Each Friday Chris Titus CZT, Administrator of this Facebook group, presents a tangle for us to focus on. The rules are that you must include the focus tangle using only a 3½" square white tile, black ink, and graphite pencil — no color, no ZIAs, and no other tile sizes. It is very interesting to see how people use the featured tangle on their tile. It reminds us that working black on white is every bit as dramatic and interesting as tiles with color.

The Official Zentangle Site: *www.Zentangle.com*

This is a the official site where you can sign up for Rick and Maria's newsletter and check to see if there are any CZTs in your area. The site lists all of the official Zentangle products available for purchase
(*NOTE: Your local CZT may also sell some of these products*).

TanglePatterns: *www.tanglepatterns.com*

This website is a treasure trove of tangle patterns compiled by Linda Farmer CZT. When I am looking for step-outs for a particular tangle, this is the first place I look. Patterns are listed alphabetically. In addition to patterns, there are tabs for stories discussing how Zentangle changed someone's life; hundreds of strings you can use to create your art; tutorials with techniques and ideas for tangling; and various video instructions. She also has a directory where you can search for tangles by type or by the name of the pattern's contributor.

4. Online videos:

YouTube instructional videos about tangling by Ellen Wolters

Ellen demonstrates the step-outs for many different tangles. Her videos also include ways to shade the tangles, which I have found to be enlightening. If you struggle with the step-outs and/or the shading of a particular tangle, Google it along with Ellen's name and see if she has produced a video of that tangle. If not, you can request that she create a video for that tangle.

5. Paper:

The Official Zentangle Tiles

These may be available from your local CZT or you can order them at the official Zentangle website: *www.Zentangle.com*.

Strathmore Mixed Media Paper, Bristol (Vellum) Paper

These papers are available at nationally known arts and craft stores and online. I like to use these papers when I plan to use colored pencils.

Stonehenge Art Paper

I recently started to use Stonehenge Art Paper after some of the CZTs talked about how much they liked it. It is 100% cotton fiber, machine-made fine art paper made in the United States. Although it comes in colors, I prefer white. To use it, you need to cut it into the size that you prefer to use. It is available at stores that sell fine art paper and on the Internet.

Play Books

I like the inexpensive sketchbooks to play. I recommend that the book be at least 8½" by 11". For more information about the Play Book, refer to *Chapter 5: Play, Play, Play* and to *Tip 22: Keep a "Play Book."*

6. *Pens:*

Pigma® Micron® pens by Sakura

Zentangle art is drawn using a Micron 01 pen. I use an 05 or 08 to fill larger areas with solid black ink. These pens are available at nationally known arts and craft stores, online, and from your CZT.

Pentel® EnerGel® Needle Tip .05 pens

I use this pen for playing in my Play Book. You can find it in office supply stores or online.

7. *Miscellaneous*

Plastic sleeves to hold tiles

I buy my tile holders at *www.cropstop.com*. The plastic sleeves fit in a three-ring binder so I can preserve a history of my progress. There are 6 pocketsvto a page. By putting the tiles back to back you can store 12 tiles per page. When you get to the website, do a search on "Zentangle Tile Pocketz" to bring up photos of the holders. Make sure you order the set that holds *tiles*. (They offer "pocketz" for ideas and patterns, and it says "Not for Tiles" after the title.)

Zondoms™

These plastic sleeves, designed to protect individual tiles, are the brain child of Chris Titus CZT and are available in two sizes. Zondom frames are available, also, and all can be purchased through Etsy at *www.etsy.com/shop/zondoms*.

APPENDIX B

Where are the "mistakes?"

Did you find the "mistakes" in the three tiles shown in *Tip 9: Don't throw away any tiles.*

The point of this exercise is to show you that, while you might be aware that you created unintentional marks on the page, people looking at your work will probably not even notice them.

In Tile 1, below, the pattern around the outside repeats the tangle patterns Betweed, Pokeleaf and Pokeroot. The patterns Ennies and Stipping go in the center. But in the lower left section, in the eight o'clock position, Ennies was placed in the section intended for Betweed.

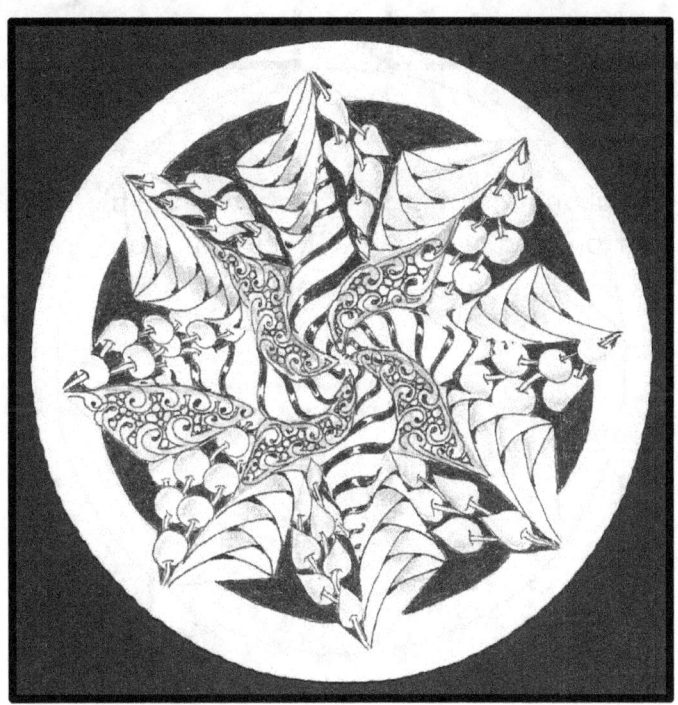

When drawing Tile 2A, below, the intention was to draw the tangle Twing across the middle of the tile. The top section of the tangle Twing is filled with orbs and the bottom section is filled with lines, which is shown in Tile 2B.

In Tile 2A the pattern was drawn with the orbs and lines alternating up and down. Because the drawing doesn't look exactly like the original tangle, we may think that we "made a mistake." Actually, it is not really a mistake, it is just a variation, which is call a tangleation.

If the viewer is unfamiliar with this tangle, he or she will never know that it is inaccurate.

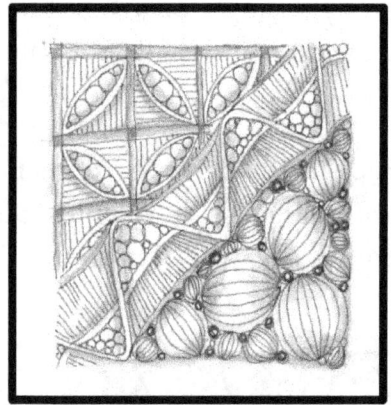   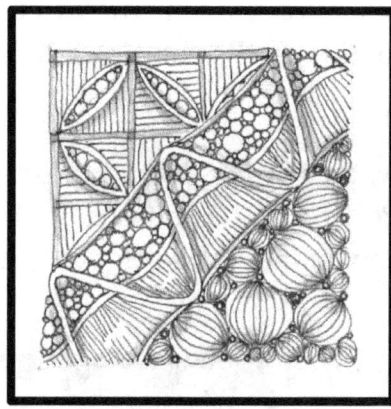

Tile 2A   **Tile 2**B

Tile 3, below, shows Tripoli in the upper right section of the tile. In each corner of each triangle there is a dot surrounded by an aura. If you look closely you will find that some of the auras are missing. Look just above the tangle Flux and in the upper right-hand corner of the tile.

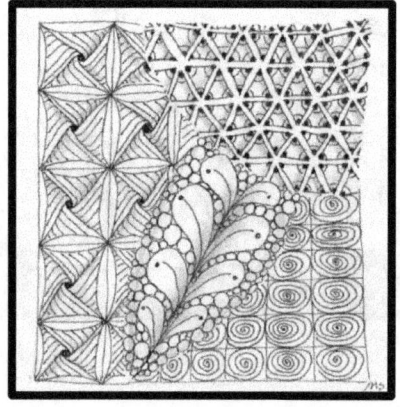

Tile 3

APPENDIX C
Tangle Credits

I would like to give credit to those who created the tangles used in the tiles shown in this book. *(NOTE: All of the tangles listed as Zentangle® - official tangles were created by Maria Thomas, Rick Roberts, or the staff at Zentangle, Inc.)*

After TOC	Crazy Huggins & tangleations	Zentangle - original tangle
Page iv	*Petals*	
	Printemps	Zentangle - original tangle
	Florz	Zentangle - original tangle
	Crescent Moon	Zentangle - original tangle
	Cluster	Maureen Stott, CZT
	Tripoli	Zentangle - original tangle
	Fugu	Sonya Yencer, CZT
	Purk	Zentangle - original tangle
	'Nzeppel	Zentangle - original tangle
	Flower Center	
	Marasu	Zentangle - original tangle
	Leaves	
	Shattuck	Zentangle - original tangle
Page 8	Crescent Moon	Zentangle® - original tangle
	Hollibaugh	
	Cadent	Zentangle - original tangle
	Quipple	Zentangle - original tangle
		Zentangle - original tangle
Page 10	Flwr Box	Kathy Barringer, CZT
	Trivet (tangleation)	Nancy Newlin, CZT
	B'Dylan	Mary Beth Schoonover, CZT

With Gratitude

Thank you to my family — my sons Jonathan and David; my brother Lou and his wife Mary Kate and my brother Doug and his partner Laurie — all of whom have, and still do, offered endless inspiration and encouragement. I love you all!

I would like to acknowledge Karen Olander, who edited the book with a keen eye for details and consistency along with a superb knowledge of grammar; Cari Camarra and Donna Cyr who patiently acted as my cheerleaders, photographers, models, book reviewers, and "Crash Test Dummies" for the exercises in the book; the other CZTs who reviewed the book - Kelly Barone, Tracy Lake, Chari-Lynn R. and Brenda Shaver. Chris Titus and Marianne McAllister for their willingness to guide me about photos and their ability to improve them; Dr. Minette Riordan and Cris Letourneau, both of whom are published authors. Minette guided me through the publishing process and offered great suggestions. Cris not only helped me with the publishing process but offered valuable suggestions for the text and graciously wrote the Foreword to the book. I am so grateful for your collective contributions to this book to make it the best that it can be.

And a huge thank you, my readers. I am so grateful that you are embarking on this journey with me.

About the Author

Maureen Stott has had many careers in her lifetime including many different aspects of teaching and training. She has taught every age group. She was an elementary school music teacher, a nursery school teacher, a corporate trainer for a software company, faculty member at a massage therapy school, and has taught a number of different adult education classes.

Her brothers were Maureen's first students when she was the "teacher" and they were her "students" in the basement of their home. That passion continued throughout her adult life and she is the first to tell you that she learns something new from every class she teaches. She has a BS in Music Education, an MA in music, is a licensed massage therapist, and CranioSacral therapist.

In addition to her teaching, she has been a Financial Aid Counselor, professional calligrapher, technical writer and editor, and script writer.

Although she retired from the massage school, she teaches her Zentangle Art classes in Vernon, CT where she also maintains a private massage therapy and CranioSacral therapy practice. You can contact her at: *Maureen@TaoOfTangling.com.*

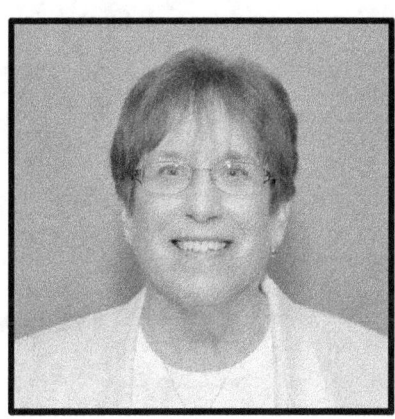

www.ingramcontent.com/pod-product-compliance
Lightning Source LLC
Chambersburg PA
CBHW080946170526
45158CB00008B/2388